PLEDGE
& PLAY

ANNE FRITSCH
PLEDGE & PLAY

How the Passion Play
in Oberammergau
Changes a Village
and Impacts the World

Translated by James J. Conway

Theater der Zeit

Anne Fritsch
Pledge and Play
How the Passion Play in Oberammergau Changes a Village and Impacts the World

© 2022 by Theater der Zeit

Publisher: Theater der Zeit, Harald Müller
Winsstraße 72, 10405 Berlin, Germany
www.theaterderzeit.de

Translation: James J. Conway
Editorial: Nicole Gronemeyer
Design: AMEN Gestaltung, www.soseies.com
Images:
Annelies Buchwieser: p. 63
Arno Declair: p. 42, 47
Anne Fritsch: p. 19, 77, 81
Gemeindearchiv Oberammergau: p. 65
Jenny Greza: p. 15
Christoph Leibold: p. 53, 115
Brigitte Maria Mayer: p. 90
Dieter Mayr: p. 10, 27
Gabriela Neeb: p. 106
Sebastian Schulte: p. 6, 31, 67, 95, 105, 110, 122, 125, 130, 133, 135, 139, 159, 161, 174, 177
Andreas Stückl: p. 36, 144, 151, 155

Printed in the USA
In keeping with environmental standards, this book was produced without chemicals that are harmful to the environment, to water and to health; there is no shrink-wrap film and all paper is FSC-certified.

ISBN 978-3-95749-391-0 (Paperback)
ISBN 978-3-95749-393-4 (ePDF)
ISBN 978-3-95749-392-7 (EPUB)

For

Emma & Anton & Robert

CONTENT

Once you get to the end you can start all over again,
because the end is the beginning of the other side.

Karl Valentin

PROLOGUE

Every ten years, people in a village in southern Bavaria stop cutting their hair for a year and a half. They do this to imitate the Crucifixion of Christ. They have been doing this for almost 400 years. Which sounds odd, but this is an event which attracts interest well beyond the region and, in 2014, was registered as an example of "Intangible Cultural Heritage": the Oberammergau Passion Play. Almost half a million people from all over the world make a pilgrimage to the foothills of the Alps each Passion Year to witness this spectacle. And the play is by no means over the hill; the cast for 2022 is the youngest in its history, the motivation on the ground is greater than ever.

I was eleven years old when I first heard that there was a Passion Play in a village called Oberammergau. It was 1990, the year in which Christian Stückl became director for the first time. I didn't know that then. I was sitting in a beer garden in Munich with my family. At the Chinese Tower in the Englischer Garten. A friend of my parents said that she would be going to Oberammergau in the summer to attend the Passion Play, which only takes place every ten years. Everyone knew what she was talking about except me. I didn't ask. But something stuck in my head. This "only every ten years" and this "the whole village takes part". It was another twenty years before I would see the Passion Play for myself. I studied. Theatre studies, German, and Jewish history, then cultural journalism. I was no longer thinking about the Passion Play; the 2000 play came and went without me noticing. Then in 2010 I was working as a theatre critic, and Christian Stückl had been appointed Creative Director of the Münchner

Volkstheater. Through him, Oberammergau came back into my thinking; the mountain to the prophet, more or less, or: the play to the critic. I got an invitation to the première. It was May, and the weather was cool as the shuttle bus left the ZOB, the central bus station in Munich. We weren't elegantly dressed; this was more like an excursion to the mountains, with thermals, warm jackets and thick socks. And that's exactly what it was: an excursion to the mountains. On the Autobahn to Garmisch it began to

A trip to the Passion Play is also an excursion into the mountains.

snow. In the theatre, where the auditorium is covered but open to the stage, it was bitterly cold. They distributed red fleece blankets at the entrance, a perfect match for the robes of the cardinals sitting next to us in the audience.

This première was an extremely solemn affair. You could really sense that this village had waited ten years to perform the story of the Passion of Christ again. Beforehand I wasn't really sure what to expect – a large-scale amateur play, I guessed. What I hadn't expected (besides the unbelievable cold) were the choir, the orchestra, the sets. The professionalism. I was overwhelmed. And I, having had religious education in elementary school but coming from a non-religious household, learned a great deal about the last few days in the life of Jesus. As Christ, played by Frederik Mayet, hung half-naked on the Cross for what felt like an eternity, while I was shivering from the cold on my seat despite the second pair of socks I bought at the local drugstore during the break, I thought it would be another miracle if he didn't get pneumonia.

Before he was taken off the Cross I resolved never to miss the play again; I wanted to be there again in ten years' time. I wanted to find out what really went on in Oberammergau. Why they all take on so much for this piece of theatre. What motivates them. Where their enthusiasm comes from. Is it religion or theatre that they believe in, that holds them together? From where do they draw the professionalism with which they approach their Passion? What are the stories behind the play? How do they come about? How have they changed over the centuries? How has the village changed?

About a year before the première scheduled for 2020, I started following the preparations for the play, wrote a blog for the Passion Play, attended rehearsals and spoke to many people in

Oberammergau. And the more they told me, the more fascinated I was by all the stories surrounding this centuries-old tradition. Just how much these communal performances define the life of the village. How people plan their lives according to the Passion. The relevance it has. These days you might say: the theatre is of systemic relevance here. As the plague raged through Upper Bavaria (the mountainous region of southern Bavaria bordering Austria) and Oberammergau in the 17th century, the villagers sought salvation through theatre. They vowed to perform the Passion of Christ every ten years to ward off the deadly disease. It is said that no one died of the plague in the village from that moment. And something of this belief – that theatre can save the world – has remained with the villagers to this day.

Now, as I write this, the 2020 Passion Play has been cancelled and pushed back to 2022. Another plague has brought the rehearsals to a standstill two months before the première: the coronavirus. Because Oberammergau represents the opposite of quarantine, of social isolation. Oberammergau means theatre that goes all in or not at all. Where everything is on stage and plenty of everything: orchestra, choir, old people, young people, children, animals … a theatre without limits – and without distancing.

Shortly after the cancellation of the 2020 Passion, I spoke to Christian Stückl on the phone. It was the time of lockdown when people were left to fend for themselves from one day to the next. When suddenly the word "home" was set before all manner of words. Home office, home schooling, home entertainment. When all at once, everything that generally happened outside had to take place at home. Except maybe home theatre, which only works to an extent (which became apparent once the initial streaming frenzy wore off). And certainly not home Passion Play. The director, normally so tireless and enthusiastic, sounded dejected, sad. But by the time we finished our call he was already looking ahead again. Passion 2022 wouldn't just be a delayed Passion 2020. Once again he and his team were going to look at the world anew, a world that was changing so much. We still don't know where it's heading. The knowledge that the Passion Play has existed for almost 400 years, that it survived the Reformation, the Spanish flu and two world wars, that it has endured crises of legitimacy and even more vehement arguments in the village helps to puts things into perspective these days. Somehow, it always goes on. This, too, is a message of the play, one which emerged from a severe crisis and which has used crises of all sorts as an engine for further development. And so writing this book means taking heart at a time when the world is standing still.   (*Easter 2020*)

OBERAMMERGAU.
A COMPLETELY NORMAL VILLAGE?

Octagon 2019. I'm on the train to Oberammergau with a croissant and a thermos full of tea, on one of my first research trips to the Oberland region of Upper Bavaria, and I have appointments for all sorts of discussions. It's a sunny autumn morning. There's no Covid-19 yet, the première of the 42nd Passion Play is scheduled for May 2020, the invitations have been sent, most of the tickets have been sold. Oberammergau is in preparation mode. The set designer Stefan Hageneier will guide me through the Passionstheater and the workshops, showing me his designs and the stage. Markus Zwink, the musical director, will explain to me how he deals with a musical legacy which stretches back for centuries, and why the children in Oberammergau get free music lessons. I will get to know Monika Lang, sitting in her living room as she explains how she and her fellow campaigners fought for years, or rather decades, for equal rights for women in the Passion.

Oberammergau via Unterammergau

From Munich you take the regional train to Murnau, along the shores of Lake Starnberg, heading south. It's work, but it feels more like an excursion. Out of the city and into the Oberland. The sun is glinting off the lake, on the train I am surrounded by hikers and mountaineers. In Murnau, I change to the small shuttle train – tiny, really – that will take me to my destination. With the waters of the Staffelsee on one side and the flat expanse of the Murnauer Moos on the other, the train makes its way to Bad Kohlgrub, then along the River Ammer, through Unterammergau before arriving at Oberammergau. In a journey of 37 minutes, the train travels through a landscape which looks as though it were affixed to a model railway. Meadows, trees and hills. The Alps gradually rearing up in the background. Outside it's autumn, with everything glowing green, yellow and orange. Travelling up into the mountains, the sky seems closer somehow. Plenty of nature, grazing cows and sheep, the occasional deer and birds of prey. Ski runs carve down the slopes into the valley. Little more. Until the train, and with it the romance, comes to a halt in the Oberammergau rail terminus next to the parking lot of a discount supermarket.

The Passionstheater is not far. A little way down the street, over the Ammer, left into the centre. "Passionsspiele 2020" is

The Passionstheater is in the centre of Oberammergau. It is a unique feature and a meeting place in the village.

written in large letters on the façade of the administrative office. All is quiet on this Monday, everyone is going about their business with barely a tourist to be seen. It is hard to imagine that during the Passion Play season, the village sees visitors arriving at the rate of 5,000 a day – equivalent to the entire population of the village. In a whole season they amount to half a million. That's almost twice as many visitors as the Salzburg Festival, eight times as many as the Bayreuth Festival and nearly as many as the Bavarian State Opera gets in a whole year.

In 2019 (the year before corona), 8.8 million tourists came to Munich – around 24,000 per day. Around five times as many as Oberammergau receives on a Passion performance day. Only Munich has 280 times the inhabitants, an area ten times as large. Proportionate to the population of the place, Munich would have to receive 1.4 million guests in a single day to reach Oberammergau dimensions. While Munich has 77 tourists per square kilometre per day, there are 167 in Oberammergau. So it is no wonder that the preparations here are already in full swing in the year prior to the Passion. Hotels, guest houses and private rooms are being renovated and spruced up, streets are being levelled, parking spaces for cars and buses are being planned.

On the day of the première, the remote village transforms into a bustling, international location for around five months. In the 19th century, the Passion Play became a popular destination for international tourists. There was particularly high demand for the "Oberammergau Passion Play" from Anglo-Saxon and North American regions. Leopold Höhl describes this in his "Guide to the Ammergau Passion Play" in 1880 as follows: "Oberammergau. For years the stream of travellers rushes past you, […] only a few, the true nature enthusiasts, come to visit. And then – all of a sudden your name fills half the world, all of a sudden the stream leaves its accustomed bed and directs its course to your quiet huts, as if some mysterious invisible power had led it there. And it is a power that lures all those thousands, educated and uneducated, city-dwelling and country folk, into the magic circle [...] The Passion Play is the destination for thousands of their journeys and pilgrimages."[1]

What happened? The Bavarian Alps, and with them Oberammergau, started experiencing greater popularity with British tourists around 1840. Horse-drawn omnibuses, new railway lines and the construction of the road from Ettal made the village more accessible. The real shift, however, came when English travel entrepreneur Thomas Cook discovered the Passion Play as a destination and promoted it on a large scale, "offering package tours and pilgrimage packages that were so popular that contemporary reports teem with American and British visitors".[2] In 1970 Lufthansa even made Oberammergau the focus of its transatlantic advertising.

To this day, numerous American travel companies put together package tours around the Passion Play. You can choose between "Munich, Salzburg & Vienna with Oberammergau" in eight days, "Bavarian Highlights with Oberammergau" in nine, "Catholic Central Europe with Oberammergau" in nine or "Grand Catholic Italy with Oberammergau" in thirteen days. In addition, there are plenty of individual travellers who book the packages with overnight stays offered by the theatre, as well as day trippers from the surrounding area. The organisers estimate that sixty to seventy percent of the guests in 2010 came from abroad. Even the most theatre-averse villagers cannot escape this hubbub. And of course very few want to. For hotels, souvenir shops and restaurants, the première in May marks the start of a peak phase that ends with the last performance in October.

But even outside the season, the Passion is omnipresent in Oberammergau. The first Jesus I encountered that day is painted on the wall of a house. He hangs on the Cross above a barren landscape, below him the mourning Mary, her sister and Mary Magdalene. A suggestion of Jerusalem in the background. On another house you can see the villagers of 1633 making their oath with their fingers pointing at the sky, while next to them, Jesus is raised on the first Cross. *Lüftlmalerei*, this technique for decorating façades with paint applied to plaster while it is still damp, may well have been invented here. It probably got its name from the house of the Oberammergau façade painter Franz Seraph Zwinck: "Zum Lüftl". All sorts of things were painted on the houses: columns and other architectural decorative elements as well as rural and Christian motifs. The longing to capture sacred events in images is omnipresent in Oberammergau. Everywhere you look there are crucifixes and depictions of the Crucifixion from many centuries, painted on façades, worked into numerous wood carvings sold as souvenirs, in the church and in the cemetery, in a variety of forms from naturalistic to abstract. There is a high Jesus density in Oberammergau.

In general, it is an affinity for art in the broader sense that makes Oberammergau special. Agriculture is secondary; the climate is harsh, the soil infertile. Oberammergau is not a farming village. I never saw a single tractor on any of my visits. Instead the townscape is determined by the three main trades: wood carving, Passion Play and tourism. And these three are inextricably linked. To a certain extent, the wood carving was a prerequisite because it meant there were always enough creative people on hand to put the play together, to design stage sets and props. The play in turn

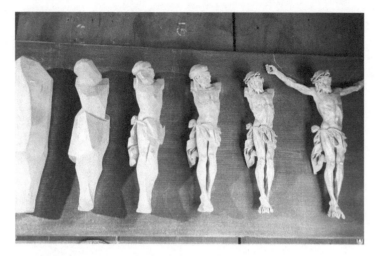

Wood carving is where it all started. Oberammergau boasted wood sculptors long before it hosted theatre.

boosted international tourism. And travellers like to take a carved crucifix home with them.

The carving is even older than the Passion; it is, so to speak, the root of everything. The men of Oberammergau who initiated the Passion Play were wood carvers. They did not come to art through the Passion, rather they came to the Passion through art. The image of performing peasants may be tempting, but it is completely wrong. This was made clear by the British explorer Sir Richard F. Burton, who visited the Passion Play in 1880; his report of his experiences in Upper Bavaria is condescending yet amusing: "English writers add to the wonders of the Passion Play by representing it as the work of unlettered peasants in a remote mountain village. So far from being peasants, the performers are mechanics, intelligent and, after a fashion, educated men. I might also call them artists. They have been wood-carvers for generations; their works have travelled over Europe to North America, and their village has its School of Design, &c."[3] At the time, the "State Vocational School for Wood Sculptors Oberammergau", as it is called today, had just been founded. It preserves the tradition of wood carving to the present day, even if most of its students now come from outside the village.

As early as the 16th century, Oberammergau's wood carvers would set off towards Italy to sell their carvings. The village was conveniently located on the trade route from Augsburg to Venice, and it had international connections. Cross-border sales channels soon developed, trading houses were established. Sculptures and wooden toys supported numerous families. Generations of villagers carved crucifixes and saints, shared their lives with biblical figures, interpreted them again and again and gave them three-dimensional faces. They showed great self-confidence in representing their guild to the outside world. In 1923 a fourteen-member delegation from Oberammergau, led by Jesus actor Anton Lang, travelled to the USA to promote the Passion, as well as their carving and pottery work. The inflation at that time meant there was "neither money nor work in the village".[4] They wanted to gain exposure for their own products through an exhibition in America, to win customers and tap into a new sales market.

They were on the road for six months and were even received at the White House by President Calvin Coolidge on 15 March 1924, posing for a group photo on the west side of the building. "The President shook hands with everyone, spoke a few words and said that he had already heard about Oberammergau from a friend, that he was happy to welcome us to his country and wished us good luck for our exhibition," Lang wrote in his memoirs.[5] Nevertheless, "some newspapers spoke of an ungracious reception of the Oberammergauers by the president".[6] The very next day, President Coolidge wrote a letter of apology to Anton Lang. White House regulations only allowed public speaking before foreign diplomatic delegations. "It was for that reason alone [...] that I was unable to have any further addresses," explained Coolidge.[7]

This is remarkable. A group of men come from a small mountain village in Upper Bavaria to the USA and are welcomed by the President. And at the sign of the slightest discord, he formally apologises for the misunderstanding. The chutzpah that the delegation brought to the White House was not accidental, says Ulrike Bubenzer, who works at the Oberammergau Museum. "This self-confidence has developed here over the centuries, most likely because of the Passion Play, its popularity and the prominent guests." The people of Oberammergau are creative, enterprising and stubborn. And yes, they also pride themselves a little on what they have achieved. Which brought them envy and the unfriendly name of "Oberammergauner" in the surrounding area (incorporating the word *Gauner*, meaning rogue or villain). And at times the Passion was the subject of fierce arguments in the village. This is a place where they're confident about defending their opinions – and disinclined to back down when others disagree.

Profane and sacred

Otherwise, Oberammergau is a not-that-small village which at first glance looks like many others in Bavaria. A mixture of the profane and the sacred, the ugly and the beautiful, kitsch and church, concrete and nature. It is framed by rugged mountains like the Kofel, which rises like a single tooth behind the village and looks as if it had arrived there by mistake. Lion Feuchtwanger, who came to Oberammergau in 1910, maliciously called it the "billboard mountain". "The high Alpine character of this mountain turns out to be a deception; only the side facing the village is rugged and massive, the whole mountain is five hundred metres high and disappears the instant you move away from Oberammergau."[8] Feuchtwanger most likely didn't hike up the Kofel, otherwise he would know that the billboard here definitely offers what it advertises. Although only 1342 metres high, the Kofel has some quite craggy, mountainous sections on the last stretch to the summit.

A lot has happened in the village in the last century; not everyone who lives here now is Upper Bavarian or Catholic from way back – not at all. Over the decades, many people from different parts of Europe and the world have come to Oberammergau. And since membership of the Catholic Church is no longer a requirement for participation in the Passion Play (more on that later), the number of people leaving the Church has increased here too. The fact that opening up to people of different faiths, or no faith, was not initially met with enthusiasm among some of the population – that's hardly unique to Oberammergau. In 1900, when Carsten Lück became the first Protestant to play a leading role, a number of people saw it as the beginning of the end.

In fact, the opposite was true; the supposed end actually brought a new beginning. Now, everyone who has lived in the village long enough is allowed to participate and nobody is excluded because of their beliefs (or lack of belief), and this is the condition under which the centuries-old tradition has become a 21st-century project supported by the entire village community. A changing society needs changing rules. And a theatre production of this size needs a majority to support it. If all non-Catholics were excluded, it would hardly be as popular as it is today.

The Passionstheater, which is apricot-coloured and dispro-portionately large compared to the other buildings in the centre, also helps define the look of the village. Along with all the cruci-fixes, it's an everyday reminder of the play. In addition, the names of houses and streets refer to the Passion, its locations, figures and past greats: Am Kreuzweg, Dedlerstraße, Judasgasse, Pater-Ros-ner-Straße ... There is even a Kaspar-Schisler-Gasse, named after the man who supposedly brought the plague to Oberammergau and who is said to have initiated the Passion Play. The arts and crafts centre is housed in the "Pilatushaus", the swimming pool can be found in the "Himmelreich", or "Heavenly Kingdom"; a tour of the cemetery is like a journey through Passions past. They are all here, the Daisenbergers, the Zwinks, the Langs, the Stückls, the Rutzens, the Preisingers and many more. All the names that have shaped the play over the centuries: directors, ac-tors, musicians. It feels like visiting old friends, even if you never met them in your lifetime. In the parish church of St. Peter and Paul in the middle of the cemetery, the right-hand side altar still boasts the Cross to which the villagers made their vows in 1633 and committed themselves to performing the Passion of Christ every ten years from that point on. It wears its centuries well; they really tend to their history here.

No compromise

On my first day of research in October 2019, I went behind the scenes of the Passionstheater for the first time, to the backstage area and to the dressing rooms. Everything is still empty and de-serted, and it is difficult to imagine the turmoil, or *Gewurl* as they say here, that performance days must bring. Everything seems too small for so many people, the processes must be truly well organised to get everyone ready for the performance and avoid collisions and congestion in the corridors. The set and costume designer Stefan Hageneier showed me his models for the tableaux vivants, the gigantic lengths of fabric that he orders every ten years from a favoured merchant in India, the costumes lined up on long clothes racks, the armour. And the two huge wooden crosses that are waiting in a corridor for their entrance.

In the "Flügelei", (the "wingery" or wing workshop), they're making the angel wings. Not with artificial feathers, but real ones. They have already been dyed black and – because they are too short on their own – several short ones are combined to make one long one. These are then glued piece by piece onto the wings. Hageneier is a perfectionist. He insists on "genuine" materials, doesn't want fakes, as he explained to me as he gave me a tour. That's why there are no artificial feathers on his wings, although of course that would be a lot easier. But for him that would be a fudge. The wings, in shapes which are naturally inspired by real birds, have a span of two and a half metres. That's a lot of composite feathers. A lot of manual labour. The armour for the Romans is "of course" made of metal and not of cheaper (and lighter) plastic. The idea is that you shouldn't just see them, you should hear them clatter as well. "It's a tradition that we don't make compromises of any kind," says Hageneier.

And even if members of the audience are sitting much too far away to tell the difference between artificial feathers and real ones, somehow you can feel it in the auditorium, the incredible solemnity with which the play is performed. Certainly, the feathers stuck in my mind. At that moment I got a sense of why the Passion is so fascinating. The three minds behind it – director Christian Stückl, set designer Stefan Hageneier and musical director Markus Zwink – don't allow themselves the slightest sloppiness; they are determined to draw the best out of themselves and everyone else. The play is sacred to them. They don't do things by halves, they are obsessed, in a way, obsessed with the theatre. Their attitude infects everyone involved. And ultimately the audience as well. And yes, every feather makes a difference. In the attitude to the whole.

Theatre addicts

Their 17th-century ancestors may have believed in a God who could protect them from harm, but over the centuries the theatre itself has become something that (almost) everyone here believes in. No matter what religion they are, or whatever else they believe in. For some, the focus is still on religious duty, for others it's the community experience and tradition, for others again it is art – and for quite a few a mixture of all these aspects. For everyone here, however, the theatre is simply a part of their life; it might lead to heated argument now and then, but no one questions the necessity of it.

This is where Oberammergau differs fundamentally from other villages, towns and even cities – here it is the people who shape the theatre. Not just an elite, but everyone. You just can't avoid it. Every person entitled to perform, every child in the village receives an invitation to take part in the play. The invitation to perform theatre is a natural part of growing up in Oberammergau. You have to actively decide against it rather than for it. The Passion Play is part of the life of the village, a subject for its gossip. It forces everyone who lives here to deal with cultural issues – and with each other. Or, in the words of Rochus Rückel, one of the 2022 Jesus actors: "In general, the Passion is always a topic; I can guarantee not a day goes by in Oberammergau where the Passion is not talked about ten times somewhere." When almost everyone in a school class or a clique takes part, it draws the remainder in. In the pub the discussion turns to matters dramaturgical rather than political. This theatre demands a lot from them, but it has also helped the place become internationally known and prosperous. No matter how acrimonious the arguments, nobody here would question the relevance of the theatre.

And that's with a set of basic constants which hardly sounds explosive at first: only every ten years, age-old rituals, always the same millennia-old history, religious themes, amateurs rather than international stars. In spite of this, or precisely because of it, the interest of the population (and visitors from all over the world) remains unbroken; it is increasing rather than decreasing. Josef Georg Ziegler wrote in his report on the 1990 play: "The fascination for the Oberammergau Passion Play stems from the fact that it has managed to remain a *play by the people for the people*. The whole village regards it as their own affair, and they're proud of it."[9]

For the director, the challenge is not to motivate people to participate, but to accommodate all the theatre addicts on stage. Because in fact there are far too many, as Christian Stückl says over and over. Or at least: significantly more than necessary. The crowd appears in shifts, there simply isn't room on the stage for everyone at the same time. Here and there they have to conjure up an additional crowd scene so that everyone gets their turn. So no, there are definitely no problems with up-and-coming talent, with half of the residents taking part on or behind the stage. Almost everywhere, theatre is an event by the few for the few, a niche event, but here it is something in which (almost) everyone can – and wants to – participate. Here, performing has a social relevance of which city and national theatres can only dream. All across the country they struggle for attention and try to seduce people into enthusiasm through participation. For the people of Oberammergau, on the other hand, theatre has had positive connotations since the 17th century. Performing together became a lifesaver for their ancestors, for the descendants it is a community project and economic factor.

In the afternoon I take a walk to the Crucifixion group that King Ludwig II donated after he had attended a special performance of the Passion Play in 1871. I follow König-Ludwig-Straße over the Ammer and up a hill until the settlement thins out and finally comes to an end. There is a forest path that leads the last stretch up a hill, and there it stands: a white foreign body

Thousands of feathers are dyed and glued to make the angel wings. The principle is that everything must be genuine – and perfect.

amid autumn-tinged trees. Over a thousand hundredweight of Kelheim marble. An enormous sculpture which inevitably catches the eye. From up here you can look down on the centre, on the Passionstheater. If you know where to look, you can probably see the Crucifixion group from below. This crucifix is without question the largest in Oberammergau. It towers over the place where the dead Christ is as unavoidable as the play dedicated to him. No, Oberammergau is not just any village in the Bavarian foothills of the Alps. Oberammergau is a theatre village, through and through.

COLLECTIVE THEATRE.
THE PLAY AS A PEOPLE'S ASSEMBLY

In Oberammergau you grow into the Passion from an early age. The children in the village not only perform with the adults, they also develop their own little Passion Play independently, which they stage in the summer of the Passion Year. Drama provides structure here. "The Passion determines the rhythm of life for the individual as well as the community. The stages of life are marked by the dates of the play," wrote Josef Georg Ziegler in 2000. "Anyone who waved the palm frond on the arm of their big sister as a child in the Entry into Jerusalem might be an extra in the tableaux vivants the next time, finally bidding their farewells as one of the old men 'beating their breasts beneath the Cross'."[10]

Living to the rhythm of the Passion

Performing is almost a matter of honour. The people of Oberammergau make room in their life for the Passion from the beginning right through to the end, adapting their own biography to the rhythm of the play. For six months, students have themselves nailed to the Cross several times a week, and flight attendants take unpaid leave to mourn their dead son as Mary. Anyone unable to get out of work faces a year with the dual burden of profession and performance. Some come to the crowd rehearsal with a cast because they broke their arm snowboarding, others with a walker because mobility is already becoming difficult. The commitment is huge. "I've been doing theatre in Oberammergau since I was 17," commented Stückl on the occasion of the Passion 2000. "Never, in all these years, have I had difficulties casting a role […]

Many an evening I have really hammered my performers during rehearsals, but the next day they are there again to work towards our common goal – the performance, the première."[11]

They say that fewer people die in a Passion Year than usual because everyone wants to experience the big event again. And who knows, perhaps there are some who align their family planning with the Passion cycle? Of course, this cannot be definitively proven, but a look at the birth statistics since 1979, at least, shows a trend toward fewer children being born in the Passion Year than in the years before and after ... Until married women were allowed to perform in 1990, Monika Lang reports that after each Passion you could be sure of a "marriage and childbirth boom, because women just wanted to participate in the Passion. And that was only possible if they were unmarried." And Anton Burkhart, who played Jesus in 2000, also confirmed the assumption that people in Oberammergau take the rhythm of the Passion into account when planning a family. "'You don't have a child during the Passion,' as they say here. And as silly as it sounds, 'when you are born determines your life in Oberammergau'."[12] If you are born shortly before the Passion, you don't get to experience it as a primary school pupil. If you are born shortly after the Passion, you are already grown up by the time you get to your second Passion. At some point, everyone I speak to in Oberammergau will list all the Passions in which they were involved. These stories are always the stories of their lives as well, structured by the ten-year rhythm of the Passion. Here you have the Passion Years – and those in between. "I was one of the crowd as a child." "I had just met my wife during this Passion." "Both of my children were born in that play year." "That was the first time my granddaughter performed." You often hear things like this. Every ten years they not only question the story of Jesus anew, but also their own: Where was I in my

Passion is part of life in Oberammergau. Whole elementary school classes often stand together on the stage.

life the last time? Where am I now? What will happen next time? Will I be able to take part again in ten years? Who will I play? What can I contribute?

There are many things that have to be done, on and behind the stage. Leads, apostles, the women attending Mary, Last Supper servants, crying women, witnesses, plenty of different servants, the adulteress, the mob, the merchants, thieves, priests, flagellants, executioners, Romans, poor men and women, dressing room supervisors, firefighters, paramedics, front of house, choir, soloists, orchestra, the "crowd" – the list of those involved in the Passion is long. There will be over 1,500 in 2022. In addition, there are 500 to 600 children. And they all come from Oberammergau. The Passion Play is completely home-made, or locally made. This means that the entire artistic and organisational process is in the hands of the locals. External workers can only be hired for the preparatory work in the office, tailoring or workshops. For practical reasons, some prefer to work behind the scenes rather than on stage. Anyone who pushes backdrops back and forth all day is paid in full, explains technical manager Carsten Lück during a tour of the theatre in October 2020. Anyone who performs in a crowd scene, on the other hand, has to go about their normal work on the side. Many simply don't want to be in the limelight, preferring to stay in the background or join the front-of-house staff to have contact with the audience. Quite a few have specialised in their very own role in the play for many years (or decades).

Theatre of the generations

Performing together creates connections between age groups. "Since 1990, when women over 35 were allowed to perform, the generations have really come together," Peter Stückl, the director's father, tells me. "Before there were old men, but only young women. But the crowd includes everyone: children, young and old, women and men." It is January 2020, after one of the first crowd rehearsals with Peter Stückl and David Bender, one of the oldest and the youngest leading actors, and I am sitting in the theatre café, warming myself up with a hot lemon drink, talking to both of them about their motivation for performing.

Stückl performed for the first time in 1950 as a seven-year-old boy. Back then, the teacher led the class in rows for the entry of the crowd into the theatre, he recalls. On performance days, the children were exempted from class for their appearance. And since in fact everyone took part, the school was empty during this time. That was certainly further motivation to take part (since the play moved to the afternoon in 2010, schoolchildren no longer gain this advantage). "On the way back to school, it was mostly only the girls," says Stückl with a laugh. "The boys were nowhere to be found in the big theatre." His grandfather, who also performed, always gave him a pair of sausages with mustard for the performance. He remembers that to this day.

Now he is a grandpa himself, and in 2022 he will, unbelievably, perform for the tenth time. In 1960 he was the youngest bass in the choir. That was the year he met and fell in love with his wife. "We have been together since day one, until today," he says and smiles. After that he almost always played major speaking roles, several times as Judas and Caiaphas. Seven regular plays, the Rosner rehearsal in 1977 (more on that later) and the play for the 350th anniversary in 1984 – that's how you get to the magic number of ten. For him, too, the years of Passion are turning points in life, moments of personal affirmation. In 1970 he already had his three children, and in 1990 the oldest, Christian, took over direction. "In 2010 I was Annas, that's how quickly you turn into an old man," says Stückl with a laugh.

Next to him is David Bender, the youngest leading actor in 2022. If the play had taken place as planned in 2020, the première would have been three days after his last high school leaving exam. Learning during the day, rehearsing in the evening, that was his plan. To be there in 2022, he has now postponed his studies and spent a year with the Federal Volunteer Service. For him it is the very first time that he will be performing in the theatre. His mother is an Oberammergau resident of long standing. However, because he lived in Ulm with his parents for a few years, he was not actively involved in 2010. Once his grandmother took him on stage with her: "I held her hand when we were among the crowd," he remembers. "I was fascinated, but didn't notice much of the performance." This time he went to the audition to which Christian Stückl and the deputy director, Abdullah Kenan Karaca, invited the young people in the village. And he was successful

– Bender plays the angel, a role that his grandfather had in 1970. The children are part of the tradition from an early age. Many have been performing since they could walk – and if they can't yet, they are carried onto the stage in the arms of their parents or grandparents. Sophie Schuster, who plays Mary Magdalene, was there among the crowd as a child in 2010. "Everyone comes together," she says. "Grandmas and grandpas, parents and us children. When Mum wasn't there, I would take my little sister with me, she would walk with me. She was four or five, had her own costume, but wasn't officially registered yet. My Mum was a medic at the Red Cross, one of my brothers was the apostle Jude, the other was front of house. My younger siblings were all in the crowd."

It is not uncommon to have several generations together on stage; many living rooms boast a family photo in which everyone from grandchildren to grandma is dressed in Passion costumes. The "Heil dir" that resounds during the Entry into Jerusalem is something like the unofficial hymn of the village; every child can sing along. The Passion has an immense familial and emotional significance and it ensures cohesion. This also results in a collective awareness of artistic development; how the costumes looked in this year or that; who played which role when; when the play was pushed back to the evening or how long the prayer "Shema Yisrael" has been part of the play – in Oberammergau just about everyone knows the staging milestones of the Passion.

Art as a profession

The Passionstheater is at the heart of the place. It opens its doors when the large-scale crowd rehearsals begin. Even for those who aren't performing. From the auditorium you can experience how something this big is created. Here they don't work things out in secret, behind closed doors, to then present it like a magic trick on the day of the première. This theatre is not aloof or elitist, it is a public process. Over the centuries Oberammergau has become a village for theatre enthusiasts. Growing up here means growing up with theatre.

Unlike other places, art is highly important here. It isn't dismissed as "unprofitable" or crazy. On the contrary: talent is actively promoted. Music lessons in school are not subordinate to the "major", more career-oriented subjects. When a student here can sing or play the violin well, it's no minor matter. The awareness that art can absolutely be a bread-winning profession is deeply rooted in the history of the place. They don't laugh at people who want to make music or theatre their profession. To this day, the rate of those who earn their living with art and culture is significantly higher here than elsewhere. There are quite a few Oberammergau residents in the German-language theatre scene alone. All artistic areas of the Passion Play are now covered by professionals. Professionals from Oberammergau (mostly men, it has to be said; there is still a lot of catching up to do here).

Christian Stückl is successful as a director beyond Oberammergau and has been Artistic Director of the Münchner Volkstheater since 2002. He transformed the ailing theatre, which was threatened with closure, into a young, experimental outfit that even got a new house in 2021, one of the most modern theatres in Europe. The musical director Markus Zwink studied at the Mozarteum in Salzburg and at the Munich University of Music, with Nikolaus Harnoncourt among others, set designer Stefan Hageneier works in the entire German-speaking region, with Stückl at the Münchner Volkstheater, but also at the Thalia

On the sidelines of the 2010 play. Most Oberammergau residents have strong memories of appearing in their first Passion.

Theater Hamburg, the Schaubühne Berlin, the Burgtheater in Vienna and at various other theatres. But none of them would deny themselves the opportunity of concentrating their energies on the Passion in the "round" years. Their first encounter with the theatre was here, and it's something they haven't forgotten. It might be the provinces, but artistically it is far from provincial. Or as Gerd Holzheimer puts it with a touch of drama: "These people could forge their own artistic path independently of Oberammergau, but that is also a part of Oberammergau – that its best come back to the village. They go out, learn from the great masters and come home to the benefit of their own."[13]

The politics of the play

If almost everyone participates, investing a lot of time and energy, naturally they also feel entitled to discuss – and judge – artistic decisions. Everyone contributes, everyone takes part. And:

arguments abound. On the street, in the local council and among the regulars at the pub. Emotions run high. Some are keen on innovation, others long for the "good old days", when the same production was staged decade after decade, in the same costumes, and no one had any "crazy" reform ideas. One gets the coveted role, another is disappointed (or offended). If the director Christian Stückl decides to open up the play and integrate people of different faiths, many a long-time resident will see their hopes dashed. Whenever Stefan Hageneier designs new costumes, some will say they are over the top. "Of course, many people said: has the power gone to their heads? Can't they just use the old costumes?" says Peter Stückl, but immediately adds: "But that's the only way to do it. If you don't keep working at it, it becomes old hat."

More than once the village has divided into enemy camps. The play is a political issue, and Oberammergau may well have more referendums than any other municipality – and most of them revolve around the theatre. The number of referendums has increased sharply since Christian Stückl took over directing in 1990. Prior to that there had been very little talk of changes for a very long time. The last serious interventions in the production and stage design were in 1930. So over generations an impression had solidified – "This is the Passion. This text, this music, this set, these costumes, this way of staging. That is how it should be and no other way." Most of those who took part in 1990 had had a lifetime of one constant Passion. So when, as Monika Lang describes to me, the traditionalists whispered, "This is no longer our play," of course they were right. For decades, the Passion had been something rigid and inviolable and it couldn't be compared to a theatre that repeatedly questions the relevance of a subject or a text. The fact that someone like Stückl came along and approached the matter in a fundamentally different way was sacrilege for quite a few. Since he was first appointed director, there have been numerous referendums on everything to do with the Passion: on the concept and direction, on the text, on the stage design.

In 2010, for example, Christian Stückl wanted to move the play to the afternoon so that the Crucifixion takes place at dusk rather than in broad daylight. Traditionally, the performances began in the morning and ended in the early evening, when the guests would stroll through the village and stop in at the pubs. In short, they consumed. That was precisely why Stückl's proposal led to an outcry in the community. The publicans and merchants feared for their income, feared dinners uneaten and souvenirs unpurchased. They were concerned about guests freezing or even falling asleep. They pointed out that people could get lost on the way back to the hotel. But Stückl was thinking of the staging. He imagined the Crucifixion at nightfall, which would add drama to the scene, with the angel before a brazier at night. The local council approved Stückl's request, but a few hundred residents forced a referendum to prevent the night performance. But in the end 64 percent voted for the play to be pushed back. Incidentally, experience has shown that the commercial concerns were unfounded. Now the guests stroll before the performance and come back during the break. "The night performance makes no difference to our business," says bookseller Alexander Schwarz. "Now people have time before the play and during the break. Before that, they would go to dinner after the play, but they didn't wander around much in town either. From our point of view, nothing has changed."

The fact that these questions get people fired up shows how much the theatre means in this place. This play is not subsidised;

on the contrary, it's an essential economic factor, a guarantor of prosperity. This is not the only reason why artistic issues always have political relevance here. This Passion Play is basically where all other theatres want to be: at the heart of society. Everyone takes an interest in it, most of them go beyond mere observation and actively participate. But the fact that this interest also means that everyone wants to have a say doesn't make things any easier.

GUILT AND ATONEMENT.
WHAT'S IT ALL ABOUT?

The more intense my engagement with the Passion Play, the more I realise that the fascination of Oberammergau is not just the fascination for a place full of theatre enthusiasts. It is also for the long history of the play, for the persistence with which the villagers (mostly the men, admittedly) have stuck to this tradition over the centuries. Because the play has not always enjoyed critical acclaim and international recognition – not at all.

The tourism advantage was barely a factor until the 19th century, and for a long time the arts pages of newspapers did not see amateur theatre as something to be taken seriously. There were droughts, wars, epidemics, but also harsh criticism and abuse. Under National Socialism, the play was used for anti-Jewish propaganda; after 1945, international criticism of the anti-Judaism inherent in the text became louder and louder. Ultimately, in the second half of the 20th century the village was increasingly divided between those who wanted to leave everything as it was and those who wanted to fundamentally reform the play. The young people were increasingly bored by this dusty and backward event, the play was facing a crucial test. In short, there have been many opportunities over the centuries to simply quit. And who would have begrudged Oberammergau that?

But they never did. The play wasn't staged continuously as planned, but there were very good reasons for the omissions. In 1770, Elector Maximilian III Joseph prohibited all Passion Plays because "the greatest mystery of our holy religion does not belong on the stage".[14] In 2021 Christian Stückl discovered an entry in the village chronicle of Pastor Joseph Alois Daisenberger from

Oberammergau, which states that they spent 49 guilders on sending a delegation to Munich to obtain a special permit. However, it could never be proven that the play did take place in 1770, and so for now they're sticking with the official version by which the play of 1770 was cancelled without replacement.

In 1810 the play was again banned under a programme of secularisation, but this ban was only valid for one year, and it was the last of its kind. The play was rescheduled to 1811. After that, it was the wars that made problems for the play. In the third performance of 1870, the prologue narrator announced the outbreak of war between Prussia and France. Since some of the actors had to go to war, the play did not resume until 1871. The Passion 1920 was postponed for two years due to the Spanish flu and the many dead and wounded in the First World War. Then in 1940 the Second World War made the play truly impossible, and it was cancelled completely. In 2020, the corona pandemic led to a postponement. So the play was only cancelled twice in all that time, and three times it was postponed. And each time they returned to the tradition as soon as they were able.

So what is it that, to this day, binds this place to a vow taken by its ancestors – or the people who lived here 400 years ago? Many of today's villagers do not have centuries of Oberammergau residents in their family trees; they or their families only moved here much later. It is also certainly not economic interests that encourage participation. The fees for most of the participants are minor, and as an event the Passion Play could certainly take place with significantly fewer participants. So there is some kind of emotional or even spiritual connection to the play that goes beyond one's own family. An overarching, comprehensive sense of responsibility for making the tradition a success, and passing it on.

Born of necessity

A tradition that began in the first half of the 17th century. In 1633 Oberammergau was a small village in great distress. In the midst of the Thirty Years War, the plague broke out in the Ober-

Scene from the 2019 production of 'The Plague': in their distress, the villagers vow to perform the Passion of Christ every ten years.

land. As an unknown writer reports in the village chronicle: "In 1633 the plague tore through everywhere, such that we thought it would take all the people with it."[15] In Oberammergau, they posted guards at the entrance to the village and lit plague fires to deter visitors. They were actually meant to warn those arrivals of an outbreak, but in this case they were to keep potential carriers away. But they failed. The epidemic reached Oberammergau. At that time there was no intensive care medicine, plague masks had strange beaks filled with fragrant aromas and were reserved for doctors. They were nothing like today's protective corona masks.

There was also no hope of a vaccine. Those who became infected could do nothing more than isolate themselves to avoid infecting others. The parish's death register lists over eighty adults who died of the plague between September 1632 and October 1633. However, the credibility of this information is questionable; four or five pages from the death register were probably added later, Christian Stückl tells me. There were neither women nor children among them. Three pastors in a row themselves died of the plague, so this list is probably not complete. The documented deaths alone, however, correspond to around ten percent of the population at the time. There was no end in sight, the people were defenceless against the highly contagious disease. All they had was their faith – and so they did what people did in those times to avert hardship: they made a vow (incidentally, no one has ever found a copy of this vow, so the exact wording is unknown.)

Pact with a higher power

A vow is simply a promise, to begin with. But also: a kind of pact. The special thing about it is that the other party is not at the table when the pact is signed; it is a higher power, intangible. A vow always presupposes a belief in this power: "I vow to do something and hope to be rewarded for it or to be spared from harm." Those who take a vow consider its fulfilment possible, trust in the invisible counterpart. "At first glance, it looks like a cheap deal based on the ancient Roman principle of '*do ut des* – I give something if, or so, I receive as well'," as it says in a pamphlet from the Oberammergau Parish Association. But of course it is always an expression of a deep faith; only those who believe in an almighty God promise him something. "Back then when the Oberammergau citizens vowed to perform the Passion Play if the plague should stop, this was an expression of the conviction of their faith – the firm belief that God himself can still bring salvation when it seems nothing or no one else is able to help."[16]

Vows for repelling misfortune or suffering were wide-spread in the Catholic world during this time (and for a long time afterwards). There is barely a pilgrimage church that isn't bedecked with ex-votos telling of accidents, illnesses or twists of fate, of broken legs and hearts, of houses burned down or harvests ruined by hail. The person who offers a sacrifice may hope for assistance from God. This is the belief. Behind all of this is an Old Testament understanding of a vengeful God who can be appeased with humility, sacrifices and offerings (and a church that sometimes sold its blessings to the faithful). The individual would vow, for example, to go on a pilgrimage or to hold a mass. If the misfortune affected a whole place – as the plague did – the method of choice in the Alpine region was often the performance of a Passion Play. What the Oberammergauers were doing was not that extraordinary. We know of forty locations that staged Passion Plays in the first half of the 17th century; between 1650 and 1800 there were as many as 250 in Bavaria and Austria. Presumably the people of Oberammergau had brought the Passion of Christ to the stage before, just not with the regularity to which they now committed themselves.

Passion Plays are plays of suffering. Arising from great distress, the depiction of the Passion of Christ was intended to lead the players themselves to the redemption that comes at the end of this drama and which at the time was, in concrete terms, redemption from a deadly epidemic. Which they believed was a catastrophe of human origin. Because the plague was interpreted as God's punishment for the sins of the people and their ungodly lives. Drama was intended as a means of defeating the pandemic. And it worked. In the village chronicle quoted above we read: "In their affliction the parish people [...] came together and vowed to stage the Passion Tragedy every ten years, and from this time on not a single person died. Even though more than a few still had the mark of the plague upon them."[17]

It is not certain whether all this really happened as described, whether indeed no one died of the plague after taking the vows (and actually, it's rather unlikely). The original of the chronicle is lost, the content only surviving as a copy made by Oberammergau pastor Joseph Alois Daisenberger from the years 1858/59. More than 200 years had elapsed between the event in question and the document we have today. In any case, the founding legend maintains that drama brought salvation to a hopeless situation, the common project led the village out of the crisis. Is this connection causal or coincidental? That too is a question of belief. But one thing is certain: the Oberammergau theatre was never simply a pastime or entertainment. And the earnestness with which the Passion Play has been staged up to the present day is testament to that.

A drama that is performed in the year prior to the Passion to this day recalls the story of its genesis: Leo Weismantel's "The Plague". It tells the story of Kaspar Schisler, who, the legend goes, brought the disease to Oberammergau: "This village was protected with such diligent vigil that nothing entered, [...] except for our church fair; there is a man from here, with the name Kaspar Schischler [...] he went around the mountain and came through the back, for there was no watch, [...] on the Monday after the church fair he was already a corpse for he carried the mark of the plague upon him."[18]

It is highly uncertain whether he really existed at all, and whether he really was patient zero in Oberammergau. The name "Schisler" is nowhere to be found in the official registers of the deceased from the years 1632/33, no descendants are known. So it transpired that the Benedictine pastor Stephan Schaller from the nearby Ettal Abbey promoted the theory that Schisler never existed, and that instead a woman from Kohlgrub brought the plague in. Christian Stückl, however, has never heard this theory anywhere else. Nor does he believe that Schisler is a complete invention; where else would this name come from? But maybe he wasn't from Oberammergau, but just a visitor instead? Conditions back then were chaotic and confusing. "Many of the plague dead were cremated immediately, the documentation is incomplete," says Stückl. "It was probably similar to the images we saw from India during the corona pandemic."

In any case, the Schisler legend was passed on orally for centuries. We can no longer verify whether there is any truth to it. But back then, just like now, many people longed to find someone responsible, a scapegoat. They came up with a simple story: this

Schisler commits adultery with a maid in Eschenlohe, is punished with the disease by God and introduces it to Oberammergau. This adultery is emphasised both in the Weismantel play and in Luis Trenker's novel "The Miracle of Oberammergau". Schisler's transgression is considered the origin of the evil, with the plague as God's punishment for a man who has turned to sin.

This view persisted for a long time, its representation on the stage never really questioned until the 20th century. It wasn't until 1989 when Stückl staged "The Plague" for the first time that things changed. Stückl rejected the Catholic interpretation. It was the end of the 1980s, a new virus had recently emerged, which many churchmen were also calling a punishment from God: HIV. "We shouldn't be talking about a God who sits in Heaven spreading diseases," Stückl explained to me before the

By performing "The Plague" the year before the Passion, the people of Oberammergau commemorate the birth of the tradition.

"Plague" première in summer 2019. He was more interested in what a catastrophe does to people, how lost the individual is in a threatening situation. Stückl also addressed the doubting of God in difficult situations, which earned him a lot of criticism in the village. Can you even show that? Someone casting a cross to the ground because he despairs of God? Yes, Stückl thinks – still. His grandfather once told him a story about his great-great-grandfather. His whole harvest was washed away. Furious, he grabbed the crucifix which had pride of place in the corner of the room and ran into the field to show Jesus the sorry scene. "Many people lose their faith in God in the face of a catastrophe, they no longer understand him," says Stückl. It was this response to peril which he brought to the fore, rather than the search for an alleged culprit.

"The Plague" had its last première in the summer of 2019, prior to what was meant to be Passion 2020. At that time nobody suspected that Oberammergau, Germany, Europe and the whole world would be ravaged once again by a paralysing pandemic six months later. The years 2020/2021 and the corona pandemic have shown how topical the questions in the play remain today. And: how much of society is still divided into those who rush to find scapegoats and those who pragmatically strive for solutions.

Overcoming the crisis

The first Passion Play took place in 1634, the same year that the Paulaner monks in Munich started brewing their own beer (another success story which has lasted to this day). The play was a celebration to mark the end of hardship. Little is known about the beginnings, not even the names of the directors. What we do know is that the play was always performed on Whitsun, on a makeshift stage in the Oberammergau cemetery. "The graves were known as 'folding graves'; you could fold them down so that a stage could be built over them," Markus Zwink told me. "The audience sat on the cemetery walls. These were certainly strange conditions, not just acoustically." The performers performed directly on top of those who had died of the plague. So the reason the play was being staged was painfully present in every moment.

Just like the "Coopers' Dance" in Munich which lured people back onto the streets out of isolation and quarantine after the plague, this play signalled an overcoming of crisis, and an end to hardship. And like the coopers, who still perform their dance every seven years, Oberammergau maintains this old tradition to the present day, while few of the other Passion Plays have made it this far. The few that have survived, like the ones in Erl or Thiersee, hardly attract anything more than local interest. It is clearly not the vow of yore that binds today's Oberammergau villagers to the play. A promise only binds those who have made it. Nevertheless, they make it their own again and again by solemnly renewing the vow before each Passion.

"Taking part is actually a matter of course, it's part of life," Eva Reiser, who will play Mary, told me. "You don't even ask yourself 'will I take part or not?' You just do. At certain times it is more difficult professionally, but even then I never asked myself *if* I would take part, but always: '*How* will I manage to take part?'" Where does this motivation come from? Why do the people of Oberammergau do this? For a while, belief certainly played the leading role. Later, when the play began to attract believers, church leaders and heads of state, celebrities and tourists from all over the world, came another aspect – the Passion made Oberammergau, a little village on the northern edge of the Alps, world-famous, and became an important economic factor. Today the Passion brings the community healthy profits and contributes to the general prosperity. Half a million guests from Bavaria, Germany, Europe and the rest of the world arrive during the season, stay overnight, eat in restaurants, buy theatre tickets and souvenirs. The 2010 play brought the municipality a profit of 34 million euros. This economic success has certainly helped in maintaining the centuries-old tradition into the 21st century. But the commitment everywhere on display here to this day is definitely not purely pecuniary in motivation. In 1922, after the First World War and in the midst of inflation, the village faced precarious financial conditions. There was a film offer from the USA which would have brought in a lot of money and made everything much easier. But the villagers rejected it, as Anton Lang writes in his autobiography: "We didn't want to sell our Passion Play."[19] He also quotes an article in the *New York Herald*: "Anton Lang and his friends have turned down an offer of one million dollars for the film adaptation of the Oberammergau Passion Play, even though they only have black bread at home – and not enough of it – to sustain their lives. They rejected this huge sum because despite all the hardship they still have an ideal in their hearts, because they believe that their portrayal of Christ's Passion can only find the right frame for inner religiosity in Oberammergau."[20]

It wasn't the only film offer that the villagers rejected. In 1957 Luis Trenker intended to make a feature film entitled "The Plague of Oberammergau", scripted by Thea von Harbou. The American film company wanted to show scenes from the Passion Play in 1960. The congregation turned them down. "Anyone who wants to experience the Passion Play should come to Oberammergau as a pilgrim," said the official statement, as relayed by Trenker. "The village, the landscape, the people and the mountains are all part of it."[21] As enterprising as the men of Oberammergau were (once again the men were the decision-makers), they were also stubborn – and unwilling to sell their tradition to strangers.

The place and the play have entered into a symbiosis over the centuries. "After all this time you really can't separate Oberammergau from the Passion Play," says Frederik Mayet. "We really are proud of this long history and it inspires us." Rochus Rückel also sees the many discussions and quarrels about the Passion as an engine that keeps the play alive: "In Oberammergau, we mainly argue about the Passion; there are always different views – and with it the will to make your own contribution, to do it according to your own ideas."

So it seems to combine a sense of responsibility for this cultural heritage, the pleasure in the community project and an expression of faith. "A lot of things come together here," says Sophie Schuster. "The fun, the tradition. But also that all age groups come to the theatre for this event and do it together. There's a brutal cohesion there, even if you don't know everyone that well. When people discuss the Passion, you always realise how much they all care." Anyone who thinks of the play as a thoroughly serious religious matter is just as far from the mark as those who dismiss it as a purely commercial event. In 2000 Josef Georg Ziegler wrote: "On the performer's side, […] a religious identification with the narrative is a prerequisite."[22] But is that still the case? Or is the play gradually breaking away from its religious origins in a time when Christian churches are losing followers? In which a growing number of those performing are not Catholic, or not religious at all?

The performers' hearts and minds remain inaccessible to us. But in fact, many of the younger generation say that their faith is important to them. Perhaps more here than in most places. Rochus Rückel, for example, calls himself "Christian, religious". In a conversation in autumn 2019, he told me that in an imaginary "ranking" with his Catholic friends he rates himself "quite far ahead". Like many others, he had religious instruction throughout his school years and attended church regularly. But still, it was only during the preparations for the Passion that he realised how big this issue is. How much room for interpretation there is. And how much you can tie to current social conditions in the world. So yes, definitely, the practical engagement with Bible stories leads to a more intensive discussion and allows people to discover completely new aspects to ostensibly familiar stories. The play makes the people of Oberammergau "pretty confident with the Bible," says Eva Reiser. "Not because you go to church so much, but because you perform the Passion." In a documentary about the 1950 play, you can hear: "These children [...] probably know the Bible better than any other children in the world. For them the apostles are living people. Fathers, uncles, neighbours and friends."[23] But the critical questioning of the stories is a relatively new development.

The Passion requires, on the one hand, a preoccupation with one's own faith (or that of others), at the same time it raises it from a theoretical to a very practical level. When Peter Stückl was cast as Judas in 1990, for example, his wife Roswitha took a highly pragmatic approach: "He's hanged at three-thirty, then he can come home and have a coffee."[24] With over a hundred performances from May to October, this is definitely an issue. The connection between the sacred and the profane is indissoluble in Oberammergau, because everyone has to somehow combine Passion and life, because most of them fit the play into their free time, parallel to their jobs.

Passion Play in the 21st century?

The question of whether we can still justify the Passion Play in the 21st century is superfluous if you understand it as an engagement with our society. After all, questions of belief or non-belief, of the role of religion in a secularised society, but also of tolerance towards other religious communities, have caused conflicts and even wars around the world which continue to the present day. In the summer of 2021, the Taliban took power in Afghanistan, forcing people to flee the return of a brutal, fanatical religious regime. People with different ideas about freedom and faith fear for their lives. The images left viewers shaken and saddened. But you don't have to reach for such extreme examples to see that

Christian Stückl and his ensemble in Israel, discussing the relevance of religious questions for all of our lives.

there is still plenty of potential for conflict in a country which promises freedom of religion. Just think of the crucifix debate in Bavaria (sparked by a law that mandates display of crucifixes in government buildings) or the vehement discussion about wearing – or even banning – headscarves. And even with no religious baggage at all, you can recognise timeless mechanisms of power and powerlessness in the story of a man who rethinks and questions tradition, the struggle against the establishment.

The material, which has been the same since the first performance, can also be read as a human drama in isolation from religion. It deals with the last days in the life of Jesus. Entry into Jerusalem, Last Supper, Crucifixion, Resurrection. Highly eventful days in which different perspectives collide and long pent-up emotions erupt. The structure resembles a classic drama with its increase of tension toward the climax, the Crucifixion, and finally the conciliatory resolution of the conflict – the Resurrection. The focus is on generalised human emotions and experiences: longing and passion, trust and betrayal, the group and the individual, truth and slander. Mechanisms between majorities and minorities which still remain highly topical. "You can use C. G. Jung's theory of archetypes to understand the insight: '*Tua res agitur* – it is you who is the subject here'," says Josef Georg Ziegler. "Calculating opportunism assumes form in Judas Iscariot, appreciative love in Mary Magdalene, fearless helpfulness in Veronica and Simon of Cyrene, pitiful cowardice in Pilate, the separation of child and mother in Mary, the easily swayed crowd in the Outrage scene ['Condemnation by Pilate']. The Crucifixion reminds us of ingratitude, of the certainty that good will prevail, the Resurrection, the final scene of hope as the essential basic attitude of life."[25] Perhaps the success of the Passion is also due to the fact that it can be read as a parable of humanity beyond any religion.

In any case, the history of the Passion Play in Oberammergau is a highly concrete encounter with religion, its visual language and its interpretation stretching over centuries. Religious art may be well past its best, but in Oberammergau they make images of Jesus, Mary, Judas, the Last Supper, the Crucifixion and the Resurrection anew every ten years. There are also the "tableaux vivants", which illustrate biblical scenes as still images. In Oberammergau, the question "What do you believe?" is always directly linked to the question "How can that be represented?".

A little belief, a little superstition?

Without question, the Passion Play is still, or even more so today, an example of living Christianity. "[One] can only be amazed at how much talent resides in this community. Amazed also at the selfless commitment," wrote the theatre critic C. Bernd Sucher about the Passion 2000. "And no less at the consistency with which the people of Oberammergau have kept their play alive. Not just as a theatre event like any other, but as a testament of faith. That is why the participants do not bow for the applause or cheers of the audience. For them this play [...] is still an avowal of faith."[26]

Here people come together to do something that they can only do together, in cohesion. One person on their own cannot perform a Passion, you have to come together to do this. Even those who think differently or believe differently. "This is a big event where the village comes together and we don't argue, we stick together," says Ulrike Bubenzer. "You get to know people from the village you didn't know before because Oberammergau is not that small. Passion is something that gives us a sense of belonging. This is why we identify with the village to an unusual degree."

Over the centuries, plenty of rituals have developed around the play, recurring processes which structure life and provide security: the renewal of the vow, the performers' names written by hand on the blackboard, the growing of hair, the prayers before the performances and the gathering of all the participants on the stage after the last performance. These moments keep the village together in spite of all the quarrels that regularly arise, and offer stability in a rapidly changing world. The play becomes a ritual, the belief in the shared creation of something great is at least as important as the religious function. That's what Christian Stückl believes, in any case. "Many people are certainly open to the religious aspect, but the main motivation for the Passion is now acting."

Monika Lang also believes that the desire to perform has "somehow got into the genes" over the centuries, and that in most cases religious sentiment no longer counts at all. "When you have a rousing figure like Christian Stückl, who doesn't just turn up with traditional Bible verses, but really tries to relocate history in the present day, to explain it and also to evaluate it politically, that's a whole new motivation. He tells the story as an everyday narrative which has a connection with us and our lives. Suddenly a personal relationship emerges." But she also thinks that naturally everyone would like to be a little bit special; you have to be honest enough to admit that.

And then there is a sense of responsibility for the common tradition: "No generation wants to be the one that simply stops doing it after such a long time," says Frederik Mayet. The ten-year renewal of the vow also gives the play a higher meaning. In a sense, they become collective rituals of cleansing and purification.

And who knows, perhaps there's a little bit of superstition to this day? The slight fear – or at least slight discomfort – at the thought of not renewing a vow that the village has upheld for centuries?

PERFORMING = BELONGING.
ON EXCLUSION AND INTEGRATION

Oberammergau has a good 5000 inhabitants. About half of them take part in the play: in speaking roles, among the crowd, in the choir, in the orchestra, backstage. So at least every second person in town takes part, organising their life every tenth year in such a way that there is enough time for the theatre. The fact that there aren't more isn't because of a lack of motivation.

I am a guest in Oberammergau, among the men and women of the place. They receive me warmly, answer my questions openly, tell me about their Passions and their lives. And yet it is clearer to me here than anywhere else that I am an outsider. If I were to move to Oberammergau today, I would only be able to perform in the 2050 Passion Play. Because strict performing rules regulate who is allowed to participate – and who is not. Now, I am only here as a guest and harbour no such ambitions. But those who move here to live are no different. They are outsiders for a very long time. So where do the strict rules come from? Do they need them? And what exactly are the rules?

The performance right

Like the society surrounding the play, the performance right has changed over time. It is a journey of exclusion, but also of gradual integration. People of different faiths, non-believers, newcomers, foreigners, refugees – as new population groups entered the microcosm of Oberammergau and the community became more diverse, the response was often to exclude these newcomers. The mechanisms for supposedly protecting one's own by keeping the other out can be found in Oberammergau as they can in the rest of the world. Over the centuries, the history of the Oberammergau Passion Play has also been a history of targeted discrimination.

Being allowed to perform was and is a yardstick for belonging in the community; if you have the right to perform you've arrived. Until the 19th century, this was self-regulating. Six to seven hundred of the village community, which in total numbered a good thousand people, performed, "meaning everyone who could and who wanted to," according to director Christian Stückl. At the time, it was taken as read that everyone was Catholic. And that special attention was paid to the actress who played Mary. There are only a handful of female roles in the play, and Mary is the most important of them all, without question. The qualifications for this role have always been demanding. The actress was supposed to be young and unmarried. Which of course meant nothing more than: preferably a virgin. She was also meant to be able to act to some extent. Often it was not at all easy to find a suitable candidate.

Richard Burton wrote in 1880: "In the case of the actresses, who must not be married, nor, indeed, engaged, private character is carefully discussed by the Wahlskomité of twenty-four, including the reverend men. The smallest irregularity is a bar to the stage; and the deprivation is a kind of disgrace. Thus many a pretty blondine has been rejected, and hence probably this section is not remarkable for beauty or talent."[27] But the lack of suitable actresses meant they also turned a blind eye to morals now and then. Christian Stückl quotes from memory an 1880 text about the cast, which suggests that virginity alone was not the criterion even then: "Choosing women is particularly difficult, they should be pretty, single and where possible talented. This time we managed to find a pretty, talented actress. The Passion Play Committee chose a Mary who is living proof that virtue alone can do little in art."

Around 1900 the village started growing rapidly in the wake of industrialisation. To maintain ties between the play and the location, a five-year rule was introduced at the suggestion of the pastor at the time; only those who had lived that long in Oberammergau were allowed to perform. Or to look at it another way – newcomers were forbidden. The intention was for the play to remain in the hands of the long-time residents, with as little outside interference as possible. They also wanted to prevent people moving into the village just so they could perform. Interest was evidently so great at that time that they considered the potential of attracting Passion Play nomads. After the First World War, the age limit for women was officially set at 35 because there were far more women than men as a result of the war. This exclusion of women lasted for decades after the "female surplus" had disappeared. And in any case women had no say. In the 1970s, the municipal council was still entirely male, just like the Passion Play Committee, which decided on the performance right, the cast, the version of the text and all the important questions relating to the Passion. This committee consisted of the local council and six other eligible men who were specially elected. From among the men who were eligible to perform. That meant, the ones who were there to begin with, who were in charge. "Women were neither allowed to vote nor to be elected," says Monika Lang. The committee election was a big local event, and staged much like a municipal election, with voting rights, ballot papers and all the trimmings. Except that, in contrast to a normal election, some of the electorate were not entitled to vote.

Male-dominated Passion

The Passion Play has long been the domain of men. When I look at this play as a woman, I see: men. Men performing. And men making the decisions. Today these are men who do not take this for granted, who reflect on their positions and are quite open to potential female successors. It wasn't always that way.

In the end the emancipation of women in Oberammergau had to be enforced by court ruling. Until the late 20th century, women had no say and only a limited performance right. In 1960, for the Entry into Jerusalem, a very particular crowd appeared on the stage: archival film recordings show men of all ages, from adolescents to old people with white beards, flanked by girls and women, all young. For any other women there was only one role: accommodating the tourists. While the men were rehearsing in the theatre, the women attended housewife evenings with subjects like "What do I cook for my Passion Play guests?". The invitations were clearly visible everywhere in the village and left no doubt about what was expected of the women – looking after the 300,000 or so guests who would come to the play. Stay at home, make beds, roast pork and roll dumplings. The women were supposed to free up the men for performing in the theatre and ensure sales in the restaurants and hotels. The children who performed could not go to the theatre with their mothers, nor did the fathers necessarily see it as their responsibility to change nappies backstage. So every now and then it was unmarried friends of the family who took care of the quasi-orphaned children. Monika Lang, for example, was always taken to the theatre by a neighbour when she was two years old.

In the 1977 Rosner rehearsal, Monika Lang got one of the few female roles: Sin, a serpent. She was the only woman to share a dressing room with the men who played the other allegorical figures. Among them was the chairman of the left-of-centre Social Democrats Xaver Seemüller who played Lucifer, of all the figures to play in a Bavaria loyal to the right-of-centre CSU. And he asked Monika Lang why she put up with it all. The fact that she couldn't even vote for the committee, that the women as a whole had no say. The following year, Lang and Seemüller jointly filed a collective action with the Bavarian Constitutional Court: for women to vote in committee elections. It was thrown out on the grounds that there was no existing legal norm and that the Passion Play was "an age-old original Oberammergau tradition". And thus apparently exempt from any efforts to achieve equality. What about the fact that this "age-old original tradition" was only a direct and pragmatic consequence of the First World War, but that the vow of 1633 made no distinction between men and women? Nobody seemed to care.

The court cases

For the anniversary play in 1984, all women entitled to participate, which meant all unmarried women under the age of 35, were entitled to vote. A few even ran for the committee but were not elected. "Of course, that was grist to the mill of our opponents," recalls Lang. Nevertheless, everyone was sure that the women's issue would have been settled by the next play anyway. That was not the case. In 1988 the decision for the Passion was made in 1990 – and everything was as it had been.

There was one exception, however. Christian Stückl had found a clause in the performance right that said married women "can be brought in if it improves the quality of the play". To that point, this passage had only been used for singers and musicians, not for actresses. Stückl wanted Elisabeth Petri – a married mother of two sons – to be his Mary. "Because everyone in the village knew that she was an extremely good actress, the local council approved the exception," says Stückl. "And so in 1990 a married woman was knowingly cast as Mary for the first time." For everyone else, the same rule still applied: only unmarried women under 35. Lang, together with Hella Wolf-Lang and Anneliese Zunterer-Norz, lodged another suit. "We are all born Oberammergau women from long-established families," smiles Monika Lang, "so you couldn't accuse us of having nothing to say on the matter. We hired a young lawyer and lodged a suit in the administrative court. Our potential fee was set as the amount in dispute." They held information events on site and collected money for the proceedings.

Because it went from one court to the next. Right up to the Bavarian Administrative Court in Munich. Monika Lang showed

Monika Lang and her colleagues in 1990 following the verdict at the Bavarian Administrative Court in Munich.

me the bulging folders with all the court files. The village council's lawyer argued that the life expectancy of women was lower at the time. A point that, of course, also applied to the men, but that did not interest anyone. He also claimed that there were no women on the streets of Jerusalem. For them, "the threshold of the house, which they could only cross in exceptional cases without endangering their reputation" was considered to be the limit. In addition, the stage was "overpopulated" anyway, and additional women would obstruct the view of the Crucifixion. He then summed up with a quote from Livy: "Now our freedom of choice is being crushed and trampled here in the forum, just as it has at home by women and their lust for domination." The emancipation of women: a horror scenario in ancient Rome – and in Oberammergau in 1990. Misogynist statements from the past were used as a justification for unequal treatment in the here and now and read as "relevant historical and religious guidelines".

On 22 February 1990, the verdict was announced: the exclusion of women from the election of the Passion Play Committee and the play itself was illegal. It was established that, according to Article 3 of Germany's Basic Law (which serves as the country's constitution), everyone must be treated equally. So nobody can be disadvantaged. Letters were sent out at short notice to thousands of Oberammergau women who were now entitled to participate. Four hundred additional costumes were sewn, and the additional women were integrated into a crowd scene. Christian Stückl's predecessor had submitted an affidavit in court that said getting that many women on stage was impossible. Stückl submitted a statement as an objection. So he "wanted to and had to" implement it. Of course, not everyone was enthusiastic about the new regulation, and many made no secret of it. "We ran the gauntlet," says Lang.

After this verdict for equality, naturally no one could be excluded because of their denomination either. "The verdict not only applied to women, but also religion, sexual orientation, origin and so on," says Lang. So there was a second innovation in 1990: for the first time a Protestant delivered the prologue; until then a Protestant had never been given a leading role. This caused another outcry in the community. In the meantime the grumbling has died down; Catholics, Protestants, Muslims and the non-religious perform together quite harmoniously. "Which particularly annoys the Catholic Church," grins Stückl. "Until then it was a safe bet: nobody in Oberammergau leaves the church because they would no longer be allowed to perform." The opening up of the play is still not to everyone's liking, even if it improves the quality. And that matters more to the theatre practitioner Stückl than the biographical particulars of his ensemble.

Twenty years

Today there is only *one* remaining criterion: the "twenty-year rule". Only those who have lived in the village for twenty years have the right to perform. Anyone who marries into the village only has to wait ten years. The fact that the five years decreed in 1900 turned into twenty years over time had just one reason: to keep strangers, or foreigners, out of the play. With the arrival of refugees from Germany's former eastern territories after the Second World War, the village grew from 3,500 inhabitants to over 5,000. As a result the rule was increased to ten years in 1950. In 1960, however, the post-war refugees fulfilled this rule, too. So the authorities quickly agreed on twenty years to keep them out of the play again.

Stückl finds this to be "extremely long": "You can't determine integration based on the time you are here," he believes. "You come here as a youngster and you can finally perform as an old man." If you are unlucky and move to the village shortly after a round year, you have to wait up to 29 years for your first appearance. In 2020, Stückl wanted to abolish the rule or at least reduce it to fifteen years. That has not (yet) succeeded. And even Stückl himself believes that some restriction is necessary. Because the director has to incorporate everyone who has the right (and the will) to perform; right is right. "And many want to. More and more all the time," says Stückl. It is a feature of the performance right that nobody who fulfils the formal conditions can be excluded. In this respect, it is actually a democratic matter: social status, income, gender, religious affiliation or origin no longer play a role.

Women now make up around half of the ensemble. In 2010, Stückl added two new female speaking roles: Pilate's wife and the adulteress who is meant to be stoned. Still, women are very much in the minority in this male-dominated narrative. And of course the play could do with far fewer women, but also with fewer men. Anywhere else there would be a casting process. Not in Oberammergau. Here the director can fill the roles from the pool of eligible performers. But he doesn't have the authority to reject anyone outright. Even if that is a challenge. Stückl sees it as a "quality". The fact that the performing right has changed over the decades does not mean that the place is now entirely free of prejudice. "There are still reservations about the fact that Abdullah Kenan Karaca, the son of Turkish parents, is now the deputy director," says Monika Lang.

But what would be left of this play if it hadn't adapted to a changing world every ten years? A Passion Play in which only Catholic men and women (under 35) from Oberammergau re-enact an anti-Semitic text – does this scenario suggest a play admired around the world in the 21st century? Would it still be a cause for euphoria in Oberammergau itself if over half of the female population were excluded from the play due to their age? And a large part of the population because of their belief, or their non-belief? It is doubtful, to say the least. Without the reforms, the impression that Lion Feuchtwanger gained during his visit in 1910 would only have been strengthened: "Since only natives are allowed to take part in the Passion Play," he wrote in "A Book Just for My Friends", "there is a sad inbreeding which has not exactly proven beneficial for the intellect."[28]

Christian Stückl is committed to the next generation and wants to involve as many Oberammergau children as possible.

The run on the play wasn't always as big as it is today. At times they actually had problems filling the major roles. For too long the same people always played the leading roles. When they grew too old, there was a lack of next-generation talent. When all reform efforts were nullified once more after the 1977 Rosner rehearsal, young people were not exactly motivated to take part in the outdated play. A generation gap arose, one that is still noticeable today. There are significantly fewer participants in the fifty-to-seventy age group. A result of the Passion Plays between 1970 and 1984, when nobody really paid any attention to the education of the next generation, says Stückl. "We have the very old and the young."

This only started changing in 1990 when Christian Stückl launched his reforms. The line-up for Passion 2022 is the youngest in its history. Monika Lang thinks that's a good thing. "It's really important that things change. If we don't have the youth on stage and in the audience, there will be no more play." Christian Stückl tries hard to involve as many children as possible. After all, every child registered in the village is allowed to take part. No matter how long they've been there. They are subject to a separate right; anyone who is under 18 on the day of the première is allowed to perform. "Parents who take part themselves or who have been here for a while, naturally they know the score and register their children," assistant director Kilian Clauß told me. "Of course there are parents who see the registration letter and don't know exactly what it means. But then they quickly find out what's going on through the children, because they talk about it at school." Stückl and Clauß considered where there might still be a need for information. And they thought of the children's home and the refugee shelter. But everyone in the children's home was already well prepared by the time Clauß came by to answer questions. He took children from the refugee shelter on a trip to the Passionstheater in autumn 2019, showed them the dressing room complex and the stage. He explained to them what tableaux vivants are, and what the lamb at Passover is all about. "There were definitely a few who were new to the topic," says Clauß. "But that doesn't matter at all to children. They get involved and have fun with it, even if below a certain age they don't understand exactly what it's about."

It's just a different community than the ones they know from school or clubs; completely different, and bigger. "It's simply a matter of integration," says Clauß. "That is why it is very important to Christian Stückl that everyone who wants to can take part. It would be a terrible shame if they missed out on it because of a lack of information." Not that he had to do much persuading. Fifteen children of refugees were registered by their parents in 2020. And anyone who performed as a child retains the right to perform as an adult. This is how Christian Stückl-style integration works. That doesn't always win him friends in the village. A "real traditionalist", as Stückl calls him, wrote him a letter in 2020. He wanted a statement as to whether "refugees" were involved or not. He probably didn't like Stückl's answer: "They are treated just like everyone else."

Being allowed to perform in Oberammergau is a sign of belonging, a sign that you've arrived. It is a good signal that at least the minors who are new to the village can be integrated into the play. Because ultimately the preparations and rehearsals are a communal experience, a collective process which gradually transforms the place into a place of theatre. Among those who have the performance right, taking part is almost a question of honour.

It's not unusual for a performer on crutches to drag themselves on stage. If you don't take part, it's something you have to justify. But in any case – that's the exception.

BUBBLING UNDER. ANTI-SEMITISM AND INSISTENT TRADITIONS

The disputes that erupted when Christian Stückl began reforming the play in 1990 did not come out of nowhere. These conflicts had been bubbling under for decades before they burst out into the open. It was about loyalty to the past versus transformation, preserving an established staging versus reinventing tradition. Because while director Stückl treats the Passion as a traditional theatrical text, previously it seems the main objective was to preserve that which had once arisen. There is little to go on regarding staging practices in the first two centuries. The biggest turning point came in 1860, when Pastor Joseph Alois Daisenberger introduced a new version of the text. This version focussed on idealisation and psychological insight, drawing out the drama of the events. "His dramatic conception [is] based on the contrasts [...] between Jesus and his followers on the one hand, and the villainous Jewish opponents on the other."[29] To heighten the conflict, the Jewish merchants in the temple became negative agents, and a few elements were added to the template. To heighten the drama, but also to heighten anti-Jewish sentiment. In the decades that ensued this text became sacrosanct, as if it were the Gospel itself. The anti-Judaism inherent in the text was barely perceived as such, let alone critically examined.

Criticism and ridicule

The fact that this depiction repeatedly led to criticism and ridicule beyond Oberammergau barely seems to have bothered the villagers. With the onset of tourism at the end of the 19th century, many guests recorded their experiences in writing. When you read these reports there is an overriding impression that the artistic quality was – to put it mildly – not always the highest. For example: "The principal defects of the play are three – tameness, want of realism, and incorrectness of historic details," as Richard Burton wrote in 1880. "In this rosewater affair we miss the rough, nervous energy to be expected from a company of mountaineers, and which would add, by contrast with civilisation, so much power to the piece. The utter absence of local colour and of chronological truth [...] revolts the traveller." No concessions were made to the professional or critical public: "nor are these the manner of men to take advice."[30] It isn't clear whether "local colour" is actually the ingredient that would have made the play more lively and raised the quality – what exactly Burton imagines by this he does not explain in detail; presumably he does not mean a Jesus in lederhosen. And he wasn't the only one who was convinced that they could have done more with it.

In the early 20th century numerous critical visitors poked fun at the acting talents of the villagers and came to the conclusion that a play born of faith had been reduced to commerce. "It is not the fault of the Ammergauers," wrote Theodor Lessing in 1910. "If there really are people living in Paris and London who are happy to pay hundreds of marks to witness a pitifully butchered text poorly declaimed, droned and acted by mediocre and by no means naive players in a tolerably charming mountain village – well, these erstwhile wood-carvers would be fools to miss out on that kind of business."[31] Passion-bashing was a widespread phenomenon, and I could barely find a single positive voice from this period. Ludwig Ganghofer attended the play in 1900; writing to Hugo von Hofmannsthal he praised the drama of the play put on by "these high-country farmers": "And how nature plays along here in the open air! At the performance we saw here, during the Crucifixion scene, a storm with lightning and thunder swept over the theatre and stage." He also saw an "artistic advance" over the play of 1880 and 1890. Nevertheless, he could not refrain from noting: "Admittedly, when people open their mouths, there is disappointment."[32]

Anti-Semitism in the Passion

Criticism of the play was not only directed at the quality of the performances, but increasingly at the portrayal of the Jews as well. "In the history of all the Passion Plays there has always been a latent anti-Judaism," Christian Stückl told me in a conversation in summer 2019. "The Jews were accused of the death of Jesus." There were around four hundred Passion Plays in Bavaria during the Baroque period, and they were always a means of propaganda in a largely illiterate society. For centuries nothing changed. And why should it? After all, this was completely in line with the views of the Church. "Basically," explained Father Stephan Schaller in 1970, "the text was no more and no less anti-Semitic than the entire Catholic Church."[33] After all, it was only in 1959 that Pope John XXIII removed the collective guilt of the Jews from the texts of the Good Friday liturgy. Up until then the "perfidious Jews" (*judaicam perfidiam*) had been held responsible for the Crucifixion every Easter, not infrequently resulting in violent riots against the Jews who were condemned as "deicides". The fact that the Jews were held responsible not only for the death of Christ, but also for the plague, may have reinforced the anti-Jewish tendency of the play. All over Europe, Jews were accused of poisoning wells and thus bringing disease to the people, which led to appalling pogroms and fuelled a hatred that continues to this day in anti-Semitic conspiracy narratives, revived once more during the corona pandemic.

Perhaps the most problematic line in the Passion is the "blood curse". In the Gospel of Matthew, "all the people" (and naturally this means the Jewish people) cry out to Pilate when Jesus is to be condemned: "His blood be on us, and on our children!"[34] This exclamation made it clear that the Jewish people were responsible for the death sentence. It was reinforced in the Passion text: "We take it upon ourselves! May his blood be upon us and our children!"[35] On a visit to Oberammergau in 1990, the Jewish religious scholar Pinchas Lapide asked: "Why does the love of Jesus in the New Testament and in Oberammergau always have to be yoked together with the hatred of Jews to form a pairing that contradicts the Bible? Can't you ever separate them?"[36] But at the time both the Passion Play Committee and consulting theologians continued to insist on the line. Ludwig Mödl, who has been Christian Stückl's theological consultant since the Passion in 2000, says that there were still heated discussions about this line later on. "My argument became the decider; when three evangelists would be happy to do without the blood curse and only one wants it, then we can leave it out. This came as a huge relief for our Jewish contacts, because there is so much persecution attached to this line that it cannot be quoted in innocence."

The voices denouncing this anti-Judaism, which was firmly embedded in the play, started getting louder around the beginning of the 20th century. One of the first was Rabbi Joseph Krauskopf, who attended the 1900 play. He described his impressions in a long essay: "I felt as if I had to rise, and declare aloud to the thousands that crowded the auditorium, that what they heard and saw, was, as far as it depicted or typified the Jew, unhistoric in fact, false in interpretation, cruel in inference." He added that it was essentially no small compliment to the Jews that a play full of Jewish characters draws a quarter of a million visitors from all over the world in one summer. But that it was all the worse that this play reinforced existing prejudices against the Jews and stirred up even greater hatred. Krauskopf had been looking forward to the performance, but the moment it began, that joy was gone. He had imagined coming to Oberammergau as a tourist and watching the Passion as if it were any other play – but that was impossible. "The moment the play began, and the opening hymn was sung, and the opening lines were spoken, the tourist turned critic; the traveller, theologian; the cosmopolitan, Jew."[37]

As noted previously, Lion Feuchtwanger attended the 1910 play, but he was not happy about what he saw either. He criticised both the amateurism and the anti-Semitism of the performance. "The Oberammergauers are the only ones in the world who have the privilege of bringing the wonderful drama that the Gospels offer to the stage," wrote Feuchtwanger. And what did they do with it? They "falsified" the figure of Christ. "Christ's action in Oberammergau is limited to chasing the money changers and merchants out of the temple. With remarkable clumsiness the Oberammergau dramaturge made this scene the starting point of Jewish hostilities. It is the merchants who stir the crowd and the priests against Jesus, the merchants enlist Judas for the betrayal; it is because he hindered the merchants in their acquisition that Jesus suffers and dies in Oberammergau." This Jesus is not a miracle worker, but a "highly uninteresting person who gets excited about trivial, incomprehensible, insignificant things and behaves like a lamenting principal." The prose gave you a headache, he maintained, and the verses made you seasick.[38]

In 1930, director Johann Georg Lang completely redesigned the production and the stage. The opulently painted stage structure was replaced by a simple stage, which was retained up to and including the 2010 play. The staging also remained largely unchanged until 1990, with costumes only remade made when required. Only the music by Rochus Dedler was revised for 1950 by the general music director Eugen Papst. Barely anything changed in the text.

Surely the lowest point in the history of the plays was when Adolf Hitler, visiting in 1930, realised how well this play could be used to stoke anti-Semitic sentiment. For the play which was performed out of sequence in 1934 on the occasion of the 300th anniversary, Joseph Goebbels himself the promotion with posters reading: "Germany is calling you!" The old anti-Judaism, entrenched in the church, made common cause with a new, racial anti-Semitism. The plays were declared to be "of significance to the Reich". Both the then mayor Raimund Lang and the director Johann Georg Lang (his brother, by the way) were members of the Nazi Party and didn't feel at all exploited, rather they felt honoured. When Hitler visited the Passion Play on 13 August 1934, he was met with euphoria. "Hitler was greeted with a thundering, thousandfold 'Heil' in the theatre."[39] The 1940 play was cancelled due to the Second World War, but the roles were now assigned by the Nazi Party rather than the local council – to loyal party members of course, as Christian Stückl explained.

On 5 July 1942, Hitler explained once again at the Führer's headquarters why he considered the Oberammergau Passion Play to be of tremendous importance for the "enlightenment of all generations to come": "Rarely has the Jewish peril been illustrated so vividly using the example of the ancient Roman world empire as in the portrayal of Pontius Pilate at these festivals, since the latter appears as a Roman so racially and intelligently superior that he functions like a rock in the midst of the Jewish dregs and rabble."[40]

Escalation of criticism

After the end of the Second World War, calls for change became louder – and more international. Like the 1922 play after the First World War, the 1950 play was promoted as a play of peace. Nobody seemed to mind that Johann Georg Lang was elected di-

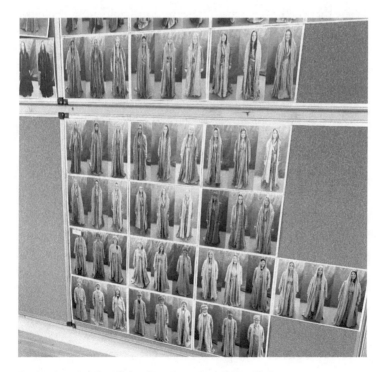

These days new costumes are designed and sewn for every Passion, a feat once considered out of the question.

rector of the play; evidently no one saw a need for denazification of the Passion. They invoked the official teaching mandate of the Church, the "Missio canonica", issued by Cardinal Faulhaber in 1934. They resolutely ignored requests for changes from Leonard Bernstein, Arthur Miller and Billy Wilder, among others. Director Lang explained: "We have a clear conscience. We have to fulfil our vow and there is nothing offensive in our play."[41]

Many took a different view. The Anti-Defamation League and the American Jewish Committee began conducting analysis and suggesting changes. But that didn't have any impact on the 1960 play, either: Lang, then on his fifth Passion, was 72 years old and not interested in changes, explains Stückl. It was not until the 1960s that there were more intensive discussions in the council, when the relatively young Hans Schwaighofer was appointed as the director of the play. He made suggestions – but they were rejected by the council, and Schwaighofer resigned from the position of director. In 1968 Cardinal Döpfner finally withdrew the "Missio canonica", the church teaching mandate, from Oberammergau because of its refusal to countenance reforms.

In 1970 the situation came to a head again. Both the Anti-Defamation League and the Jewish Committee called for a boycott of the play. Many guests, particularly from the US, stayed away. The mood in the village was heated; Stückl remembers this time as a child in his parents' pub. "There was an incredible amount of discussion among the regulars. I always sat down to listen and found it really interesting. They badmouthed the 'peasant bishop', Cardinal Döpfner, and Rabbi Marc Tannenbaum from the American Jewish Committee, the 'Jews'. You would always hear 'that shit Tannenbaum wants to ruin everything for us'."

The main problem of the Daisenberger text was that Jesus is portrayed as the first Christian to be attacked by the Jews.

Benedictine Father Schaller also pointed out the anti-Jewish elements in the play, as quoted by Hannes Burger in the *Süddeutsche Zeitung* for the première: "It gives the impression that the reason Christ had to die was because he ruined business in the temple for the incorrigible Jewish hagglers." Burger spoke to the mayor at the time, Ernst Zwink, who also seemed open to change. "I would suggest critics go to the Passion Play and form their own judgement. And then they should not just criticise, but make specific suggestions for changes. From the proceeds we will establish a fund so we can finance study assignments to improve the play."[42] He deliberately ignored the fact that there were already concrete suggestions from both Schwaighofer and Schaller.

Schaller's proposals for reform were rejected. The impact of the text was considered less important than the visual and dramatic aspects. "Schaller's proposal, for example, to remove the broad-brush, non-biblical scene of the merchants drooling for 'revenge' and spinning their intrigues, was rejected with the following arguments: first, it is the only funny scene in the play, and second, the merchant roles are important for training the next generation of Pharisees in intrigue and agitation."[43]

And evidently, many simply denied that changes were even necessary, that there was even a problem with anti-Semitism in Oberammergau. It was a defiant attitude that seemed to say: "What we perform is the Bible. And what is in the Bible is sacred and therefore cannot be questioned." In his article, Burger quotes then mayor Ernst Zwink: "We should be happy that an entire village still has enough idealism to perform such a play, and we should be happy that there is still an oasis of peace here in our radical times." And one anonymous Oberammergau resident said: "We can't help it that the whole Passion happened to the Jews. We would have preferred it if it had been the Prussians.

That would have been a lot easier."[44] But it wasn't the Prussians, no matter how much anyone might have wished it. And it certainly wasn't easy. In particular, the calls for boycott in the USA hit Oberammergau hard, especially the local hotels. Because deals with two nights' accommodation were always sold abroad, while domestic guests usually stayed for a maximum of one night or even returned home immediately after the performance.

The Rosner rehearsal

With the accusations of anti-Semitism becoming louder and louder, and economic pressure also increasing, a cautious compromise was reached: in 1977, three years before the next real Passion, they staged an intermediary version based on an older, allegorical version of the text by the Ettal Benedictine pastor Ferdinand Rosner from 1750. It was not the Jews who were to blame; instead, allegorical figures such as envy and hatred appeared as qualities that all human beings carry within themselves. Sent by Lucifer to harm Jesus, they sow resentment and stoke the mood until the Crucifixion. Although the original text also contains formulations such as "the cursed Jewish mob", they were simply removed as Christian Stückl tells me. Hans Schwaighofer directed and designed the sets, masks and costumes. These were shown in an exhibition in the Oberammergau Museum in 2021. They had nothing in common with the Passion as it was before. There were elaborate, filigree, almost Art Nouveau trees and glowing hell-fire. Sin was depicted as a snake, an oversized reptile made of fabric snaking from the actress's head down to the floor.

I only saw the models, the snake costume and a few film extracts, but this was obviously something completely different

Set model of the "Rosner Rehearsal". Hans Schwaighofer tried a completely different Passion with artificial aesthetics.

to the once staid Passion. Visually impressive and new. Too new for some. The rehearsals lasted seven months and around 700 people from Oberammergau took part. The eight performances were a success. The Jewish Community of Bavaria and the American Jewish Committee praised the performance; Oberammergau expert Burger wrote in the *Süddeutsche Zeitung*: "Yes, this Rosner is – with all sorts of restrictions in the detail – in principle not only playable but also accessible to the public; it also enables a means of representation that almost disqualifies Daisenberger as a serious alternative. Of course, this doesn't discount the fact that this rough draft, which in a short time has already turned out astonishingly well, still has to be worked diligently with saw and chisel, carving knife and file – and there is still time enough for that before 1980."[45]

Although the underlying text was even older than the Daisenberger version, the staging was aesthetically astonishing and courageous. A gamble, risky and exciting. The village was divided, with a conflict along generational lines. Many of the young people were delighted. Christian Stückl remembers how they adored the Schwaighofer. "There was a line in the play: 'Long live our Prince and Lord, long live the great Lucifer.' On the last day of the play we shouted: 'Long live our Prince and Lord, long live the great Schwaighofer.'" For him personally, this Passion was an "awakening experience": "It was Schwaighofer who made me want to become a director." He understood what staging means: to grasp a text as material. But also many of the older performers were there: "My Dad was Judas, my Grandpa was Annas."

In Oberammergau there was a state of emergency, Monika Lang goes so far as calling it a "war": "There was defamation to an extent I had never seen. The Stückls received a pile of dirt at their front door because Christian's father was deemed to be a 'turncoat'. Somebody spat on me in the street and said: 'You snake!'" Anonymous letters were sent, businesses boycotted. And all because people found a theatrical production too daring. In a public consultation afterwards, the majority of the villagers decided to stick to business as usual in 1980. "Schwaighofer was so frustrated that he quit," says Stückl. "We young people wanted to see him continue, we were disappointed."

Back to business as usual

The 1980 play went on under the direction of Hans Maier, with no noteworthy changes from the 1970 version on the stage. The guiding principle was: "How did we do it with the last Passion? That's how we'll do it this time too."[46] Monika Lang refused to perform in the Daisenberger version again, even though it was the last time she was permitted to participate according to the old women's performance right. In an article in the *Süddeutsche Zeitung*, Herman Unterstöger describes how they anticipated possible criticism in the official illustrated volume – only to reject it: "Nevertheless, people will try to criticise Oberammergau. But that doesn't matter much to the Oberammergauers." Unterstöger goes on to say that disputes with the Passion's critics had been officially settled in a "report" as early as 1970. "Anyone who objects to the form and meaning of the Passion's portrayal [must] be considered as standing outside the Christian community, as an undercover enemy of the faith even." Criticism, he inferred, can basically only come from believing Oberammergau residents. To put it another way: we won't let outsiders tell us what to do. And the self-appointed theatre and Passion critic Johannes Goldner confirmed to the decision-makers that everything was fine. "There is now a book of the text which should meet the expectations of all Passion visitors in every respect and which no longer offers any reason for attacks by outsiders." Others, such as the American Jewish Committee, took a different view. "As it is today, the drama retains an anti-Jewish tendency, despite all the well-meaning efforts of the adaptation."[47]

It wasn't just on the question of anti-Semitism that Oberammergau refused to countenance fundamental reform. From an artistic point of view, too, the majority viewed experiments like the Hans Schwaighofer production with suspicion. They shared Goldner's view "that the Passion can never be an artistic expression"[48]. They believed that it could only be judged liturgically, so from the outset it is beyond any criticism that might relate to the Passion as a work of art, as a play. Approaches like the Schwaighofer production, they further believed, are therefore fundamentally misguided. And, so the argument goes, 500,000 visitors could hardly be wrong (nobody asked whether all these visitors agreed with what they saw or were even happy).

The play for the 350th anniversary in 1984 was again directed by Hans Maier. Apart from a few cosmetic changes to Johann Georg Lang's set of 1930 (which promptly resulted in a lawsuit from his son), everything stayed the same. Numerous tickets ordered from the USA were returned. A review in the *Süddeutsche Zeitung* was hardly enthusiastic: "As expected, Hans Maier stuck to his staging of 1980, the longueurs of which are just as obvious as its dramaturgical naivete, which, according to the Oberammergau concept, may be intentional. Under this interpretation, the solemn, awkward style of declamation, the sparse arsenal of gestures, the lack of theatrically effective guidance of the performances, the mawkish directness of the tableaux vivants – all of this is an expression of the fact that one is removed from artistic ambitions, that one wants nothing but a simulated sequence of pious, worshipful scenes to fulfil a promise inherited from the forefathers."[49]

This would be the last play in the traditional mode; in 1987 the municipal council elected the then 24-year-old Christian Stückl as the director for the Passion in 1990. And by opting for him they opted for change.

THE END AS BEGINNING.
THE REINVENTION OF THE PLAY
SINCE 1990

I have only a vague and theoretical idea of how the staging of the material has evolved over the centuries. As I have gathered from reports and the few film excerpts in the archives of the Bavarian state broadcaster and from the Oberammergau Museum, for a long time the play was a retread of Christian clichés which didn't really prompt reflection, with dissemination of traditional images of the "enemy" of greater or lesser subtlety. If the community had decided in 1990 to preserve the play as it was, and to reject reformation, who knows whether it would have made the leap into the present or instead sunk into irrelevance. It almost certainly would not have become a prime example of overcoming centuries of resentment and prejudice, a symbol of tolerance and togetherness.

The election of Stückl

The election of Christian Stückl as director for the Passion Play in 1990 was a close-run thing. In a run-off election on 8 July 1987, he was elected by the local council with nine votes to eight. Hans Maier, director in 1980 and 1984, lost. He couldn't really understand his defeat. "Nevertheless, Maier does not want his successor to pay for the matter: 'hopefully he will pull it off'."[50]

As for this ominous successor, who is only named as "the son of Caiaphas" in the title of the article, because his own name is at that point completely unknown outside of Oberammergau, the author merely reports that: "His grandfather and his father each played Caiaphas twice, he himself [...] has been in the festival choir since 1977." Christian Stückl had already created theatre with "young people", it stated, otherwise he was a blank slate. "One thing is certain in any case, that he wants to 'tackle something new' and not 'reheat the old'," as Hermann Unterstöger quotes the 25-year-old Stückl.[51]

Stückl himself remembers that in the mid-1970s he got his hands on what was known as the "Black Book" which included the demands of the Anti-Defamation League and the American Jewish Committee, and he gradually developed an awareness of what it meant: anti-Semitism in the Passion. He was in the choir for the 1980 and 1984 plays – and made a note of what he would change if he were director. "It was clear to all of us that it couldn't go on as it was," he says. Despite growing international protests against the anti-Semitic version of the text, any effort at reform was undermined. The more progressive Cardinal Döpfner was succeeded in the Archdiocese of Munich and Freising by the conservative Joseph Ratzinger, who "fabricated a step backwards," as Stückl puts it.

When word came that Otto Huber, a senior teacher and Oberammergau resident in exile, would be brought from Lauingen an der Donau to take over direction, Stückl thought: "If it's him now, it will never be me." So he stood as a candidate himself. In 1986 he went to the local council and said he wanted to be the director. So there were three candidates: Hans Maier, Otto Huber and Christian Stückl. In the first ballot, Huber, who was pretty sure of his cause, was voted out. It came down to that run-off between Maier and Stückl. As expected, the reactions were very mixed. For some, Stückl embodied the hope that finally, the play would shake the musty feel it had acquired over a thousand years. For others, he was the youthful revolutionary endangering the continued existence of a centuries-old cultural heritage. His ideas for a new stage design and a new version of the text frightened a fair few villagers. One day he found a sign on his front door: "Gravedigger of Oberammergau, beat it, or your legs will get wet."

But who was this young savage, this "son of Caiaphas" who was setting out to revolutionise the Passion Play? There is something strangely fateful and predetermined about his biography. The Stückls are a long-established Oberammergau family. They didn't generally have a say in the big questions. But they are firmly rooted in the village and the Passion. Everyone took part. For Christian Stückl the first time was 1970, as a child in crowd scenes. "I was nicknamed the Stage Terror, I was always in the theatre and I can hardly remember going to school in second grade," he tells me. Once he got a slap in the face from the director because he would sneak into a different tableau vivant every day. "He said the next time I put myself where I didn't belong, I'd cop one – and that's what happened. And apparently, I can't remember it myself, I came home and said: 'When I'm the director, I'll hit back.' So my first motives were base: thoughts of revenge." Stückl laughs.

There was only one person at home who was strictly religious, and that was Grandma, the only Protestant among all the Catholics. She often took him to church with her. "I found it all pretty terrible because it was so boring. The incense, the pomposity and the theatricality of the Catholic Church – they had none of that. As a child I said: 'They don't even have smart costumes'."

Stückl liked the Catholic Church because it was one big theatre – mass with its dramaturgical structure, the dialogue between pastor and congregation, the liturgy, the Easter vigil, in which twelve candles for the apostles are lit in the dark, illuminating the room … It all seemed almost as tempting to him as the Passion Play. And so two career aspirations came to mind: priest or Passion director. Something to do with theatre, in any case. The fact that he did not become a priest is in turn related to his passion for the theatre; he was kicked out of sixth grade at the monastery high school in Ettal because he skipped class to sew the costumes for his Nativity play production. An honourable reason for truancy, and a remarkable commitment for a twelve-year-old. But he was thrown out of school nonetheless. Later he tried the "seminary for late vocations" in St. Matthias Waldram, but everyone there was "so pious and clammy" that he couldn't stand it. The fact that his career as a cleric didn't take off is certainly a loss for the Catholic Church, but most definitely a gain for the theatre. So all that remained was Passion director. A job that only exists in Oberammergau. And even there it only exists every ten years.

And since the job of "Passion director" doesn't come with an internship, Stückl first completed an apprenticeship as a wood carver. Well, all of the directors he knew had been wood carvers. But the solitude of the workshop was not his thing. In 1981 he founded his own theatre group, staged Molière and Shakespeare, and organised trips to the Kammerspiele in Munich. In the spring of 1987, Stückl and his troupe staged "A Midsummer Night's Dream" in Oberammergau. The journalist Erich Kuby witnessed one of these performances. He was apparently so enthusiastic about the performance that he used his contacts at the Kammerspiele in Munich, and the next day the theatre called Christian Stückl and offered him a position as assistant director. For three weeks he sat in on Dieter Dorn's production of "Faust", then he worked with Volker Schlöndorff, who was staging Heinrich Böll's "Women in a River Landscape". Instead of an open-air theatre with a mountain view, he found himself in a dark rehearsal room, a "bunker with no daylight". Previously Stückl had thought, "making theatre is simply an incredibly wonderful and intense form of togetherness"; then he started smoking. "Suddenly there were a whole lot of vultures pecking at each other and pouncing on the director to ingratiate themselves, and constantly vying for the Artistic Director's favour as well."[52]

He came from a theatre that was different, more permeable. "Here I would talk to my Dad and Grandpa about the theatre, all the generations among the regulars at the pub would think about what had to be done differently," he says. "We asked ourselves all the questions you ask yourself at the theatre. But it was much less uptight. Here you don't have the kind of closed bubble you have in professional theatre." That his theatrical thinking was moulded by a form of theatre that only exists in Oberammergau, that he had a dream job that only exists here (rather than just becoming any old director), informs his work to this day: the themes he addresses himself on stage and which revolve again and again around religion and anti-Semitism. But also in his way of working, his desire for shared development, his open and unerring eye for young talent.

So at first he turned his back on Munich and came back to Oberammergau. After all, his greatest task was waiting there: the revision of the Passion Play. When Stückl staged his first Passion in 1990 at the age of 27, the question of reform came up again. There were 18 requests from the Anti-Defamation League and the American Jewish Committee. Stückl read through them and said: "We can implement 16 immediately without any problems." But then people said: "We can't let the Jews dictate what we do here." Stückl stuck to his guns. "Yes we can! After such a long time of being inflexible, we have to do it now and make sure that we do away with the allegations."

The Passion 2000. Christian Stückl integrated Jewish symbols into the play, showing Jesus as an observant Jew.

The council soon put Otto Huber at his side as the deputy director – and as something of a minder as well. "I think they grew afraid of their own courage," says Stückl. His ambition was also checked on another front – the Catholic Church sent him a theological advisor. He didn't want to go as far as Stückl and slowed him down – with the "blood curse" among other things. He wasn't just reined in with the text, but with the set design and the costumes as well. And Stückl realised: "I probably have to put up with this for now, then I can really get down to it in 2000 and implement my changes." So at first he approached it cautiously, contenting himself with minor changes. He had seen from the example of Schwaighofer that they can cut you down as a director if you want too much too quickly. That was certainly how it was perceived in the reviews of the première. "Stückl and his deputy Otto Huber have helped pave the way for a more positive portrayal of Judaism, in particular by making changes to the staging. […] With this state of affairs, the focus is naturally toward the future, that is to say toward the 2000 play, and the question is, as it was in the 1970s, whether it isn't high time for a reform."[53]

The new millennium

By the time Stückl staged his second Passion in 2000, the omens had changed. He had returned to the Münchner Kammerspiele, where in 1991 he had staged the world première of Werner Schwab's radical comedy "People Annihilation or my Liver is Sick". The production appears to have been legendary. "The director Stückl brought exactly the right amount of the Catholic insider's irritability to fearlessly descend into Schwab's arch-blasphemous petty bourgeois hell in the social underground. Unencumbered by the fear of crossing stylistic barriers, he succeeded in a brutal religious mystery panopticon and an elevated Punch and Judy Passion Play," according to the critic Christopher Schmidt.[54] Stückl was named Young Director of the Year by the trade journal *Theater heute*, the "People Annihilation" was invited to the Mülheimer Theatertage and the Berlin Theatertreffen, and having been in-house director at the Münchner Kammerspiele for a number of years Stückl was now the Artistic Director designate of the Münchner Volkstheater.

So he was no longer just the ambitious son of the village publican, the "Caiaphas", but a nationally recognised theatre man. He had developed yet another new concept for the Passion, including changes to the text and a new stage design. But because the Oberammergau decision-makers are the Oberammergau decision-makers and not a Theatertreffen jury, the CSU faction announced in the local council before the director's election that they would not vote for Stückl. Their preferred opponent: Otto Huber, again. But since Stückl is Stückl, and a stubborn man, he had no intention of putting up with that. If the local council won't vote for me, the people should vote for me directly, he thought to himself. And he put his directorial concept up for election in a referendum. Otto Huber withdrew, Rudi Zwink, who played Jesus in 1980, also submitted his own concept. Stückl was elected, but a second referendum followed – just to be sure, as it were – which determined that the Daisenberger text should be performed. "I didn't want to do the Rosner at all," he says. "I didn't want to compete with Schwaighofer."

Stefan Hageneier designed new costumes and sets, Stückl and Otto Huber, who was on board as dramaturge, wrote entire new scenes and fundamentally changed the perspective on the role of the Jews. "Officially it is still the old text, but there is less and less Daisenberger in it. Thank God," says Stückl. "Otto and I were diametrically opposed in our thinking, we chafed against each other a lot, but something came out of it." The Passion Play becomes an internal Jewish conflict, with advocates and adversaries among each group, in the High Council, among the common people and in the inner circle of believers. The expulsion of the merchants from the temple, which reinforced "the stereotype of the Jewish haggler," was shortened, and the conflict with the merchants was replaced by a confrontation with representatives of spiritual power.[55] Jesus was no longer simply a figure of suffering, he was also a fighter for his Jewish faith. "The Daisenberger text is based almost exclusively on the Gospel of John," explains Stückl. "Right from the start, Jesus is put forward as the Son of God, whereas Matthew is much more inclined to see Jesus as a man and as a Jew. My aim is to bring Jesus down to earth and make him comprehensible." No longer relying on clichés and prejudices, but exploring an all too human story.

To ensure success, the cardinal and the regional bishop sent him a new theological advisor: Ludwig Mödl from the Ludwig Maximilian University in Munich. Mödl remembers the symposium with Jewish rabbis in the run-up to the Passion 2000, in which they discussed all the changes at length. "The major Jewish world organisations see Oberammergau as a symbol of the extent to which the Catholic Church and, above all, the Germans are ready to eliminate anti-Semitism and to engage with the Jewish part of Christianity in the Passion," Mödl told me in autumn 2021. Of 29 requested changes they were able to implement all but two. "It wasn't because of the rabbis, but because of the majority of Oberammergau residents; there was a passage in the prologue we couldn't change, and a rhyming passage that was so bound to the music and was pretty much an 'ear worm' in Oberammergau. Evidently every kindergarten child in Oberammergau knew the two passages by heart, they didn't want to change them," says Mödl, who also acted as an "arbitrator" between the parties. Because even though everyone, he felt, was in favour of removing the decidedly anti-Semitic passages, opinions on what was anti-Semitic differed widely. In Mödl's perception, it wasn't anti-Semitism that fired opposition to change, but insistence on tradition, "which if we changed would upset others." Mödl helped Christian Stückl implement the changes and the breakthrough was achieved.

Theatre to be taken seriously

The 2000 play would be perceived in a different league, as theatre to be taken seriously. Where Sven Ricklefs had described the Passion Play as an "ancestral folk festival"[56] in a 1994 profile of Christian Stückl, for the first time the prestigious newspaper *Süddeutsche Zeitung* sent a theatre critic from Munich rather than a local reporter. And, what's more, he was enthusiastic. "This truly difficult undertaking is a success. Because the performance does not aim to identify or exclude anyone as a Christian, Jew or Muslim. [...] It's all about salvation and faith, not about segregating denominations. [...] Jesus, the Jew, does not wish to renew. He wants to lead us back on the right path [...] It is a great achievement of the Oberammergauers that their play is never loud, never shallow, never kitsch or sweet. Stückl manages to stage a well-observed tension between the characters, even between the people appearing as the crowd and the protagonists; they listen to each other. And this interest transforms into movement, gesture, gaze.

Stückl isn't afraid of silence, or tumult. Even the flagellation, even the realistic Crucifixion, aren't presented as lurid, creepy turns. Stückl stages pain and grief," writes C. Bernd Sucher.[57]

It was a revolution from within. Stückl is an initiate, deeply rooted in the traditions of the Passion Play – and those of the Catholic faith. He had wanted to be a director since he was a child. He is not a theatre man who came from outside to revolutionise the Passion. Instead, he is a man of the Passion who found his way to the theatre through it. And even if some may have thought otherwise at the beginning, Stückl sums it up when he says: "I'm not a vandal at all."[58] For him, it's never about form, al-

Christian Stückl repeatedly interrogates the text and the story, relating it to the present.

ways about the narrative. The form then arises out of the narrative by itself. Form follows story, you could say.

Stückl does not impose ready-made theses on the ostensibly familiar. Rather, he reads and questions the text of the Passion critically every ten years – and applies what he has discovered in it, what he had not seen the last time. When he is directing, he concentrates, keeps asking questions, takes nothing for granted and constantly reinvents the old. In 2010 he was not just a successful artistic director in Munich, he also introduced a summer of theatre to Oberammergau outside of the Passion, staged "Jedermann" at the Salzburg Festival and the opening ceremony of the football World Cup in Munich – and no one disputes his post as director in Oberammergau any more. He still gets three dissenting votes; the council can't entirely dispense with differences of opinion. And since Stückl now knows the mechanisms only too well, he swore his fellow citizens to agreement at a village meeting in early 2009: "Ultimately, we can only come up with a good Passion if we all stick together and if we all know what an important asset this Passion Play is for all of us. This is very important for driving this Passion Play forward, for taking it further. That is the real Oberammergau tradition and that is why we are also […] the most famous Passion Play: because we have always dared to do new things, to go further, to change things."⁵⁹ He is very familiar with the lines of conflict that run through the village, knows very well that you can't take cohesion for granted here.

And one month before the première in 2010, an article appears in the *Frankfurter Allgemeine Sonntagszeitung*, which brings all sorts of things back to the surface which seemed to have been overcome long before. Outside the dispute over the night play is raging, Florian Streibl, member of the Bavarian state parliament and son of the former Minister President, apparently "suggested a crisis intervention team to save marriages during the Passion period. Families will be torn apart by the night play." Streibl does not let his hair grow because he cannot "walk around like a Neanderthal" in Munich. And when "half of the people in some of the crowd scenes are women, it feels a bit like Monty Python's parody of Jesus, 'The Life of Brian'." In the article, wood carver Martin Müller even describes Stückl as a "Passion dictator" who wants to turn the play into a "would-be professional theatre" and "reinvent" the Bible. "Since his council colleague Stückl came to power, they have had to ask Jewish organisations what they are allowed to say on stage."[60] Still no trace of unity, then.

The 2010 plays are Stückl's third; his view of history has changed in twenty years. This time he clearly portrays Jesus as a Jew, and also shows Judas's repentance. Markus Zwink sets the prayer "Shema Yisrael" to music for the visit to the temple, draws inspiration from both Hebrew synagogue chants and from Ofra Haza's pop music to gain sonic access to another world. "Not just the choir, but the entire crowd sings in Hebrew here," says Zwink. "It was a lot of fun for everyone and immediately became a kind of classic."

In 1990, Zwink dared to rework Rochus Dedler's 19th-century compositions for the first time. First was a new bridge of seven bars, and even that came with major qualms. "I grew up in a time when there was mostly stasis, with no major innovations in the Passion Play. Essentially there was no discussion about the text or music, which were considered inviolable." In 2000 he composed many of the tableaux vivants anew, creating a musical depth by splitting the choir. And then in 2010 the "Shema Yisrael". This is another step towards greater tolerance and openness to the world, away from anti-Semitism. Through a song – no more, but also no less.

In 2010, through colourful images and impressive crowd scenes, Stückl told of a man who sticks to his convictions and calls on his contemporaries to change their views. Of a man who is strenuous in his consistency, demands a lot from his fellow human beings and sometimes gets on their nerves. Together with Otto Huber, Stückl did a lot of work on the text in advance and added scenes that bring Jesus' convictions and faith to life, such as the rescue of the adulteress from stoning. From a story dating back millennia they drew current questions, bringing the text back to fundamentally human and moral aspects: "Let him who is without sin cast the first stone." The Jesus of this Passion upheld pure faith, reconnected his teachings to everyday life.

The Resurrection

So all was well? For theologian John Warwick Montgomery: not at all. Having attended the play six times between 1970 and 2010, he renounced his fidelity to it in an essay: "However, I will probably not visit again – and not for reasons of age."[61] What was the problem? Above all, Montgomery criticises the "shallow handling of the Resurrection which is depicted in the last scene of the play"[62]. There is no dialogue among the soldiers who guard the tomb of Jesus or appearance of Jesus from the tomb. "The Encounter with the Risen Lord" has become a "minimal encounter" in which Jesus remains silent. Montgomery dismisses Ludwig Mödl's explanations in the foreword of the 2010 text as "nonsense". "Classical theology has always taught the Resurrection as a historical fact and as visible as the Crucifixion." And he concludes: "Keep liberal theologians away from fine artistic expressions of the revealed truth."[63]

Montgomery was correct in his observations – there was no scene of the guards at the tomb in 2010. Christ no longer climbs out of the tomb with the white shroud and the standard in hand. Instead, an angel sits in the middle of the stage by a brazier and tells Mary Magdalene that Jesus is risen. She calls the others over, everyone lights their candles – and Jesus steps into their midst and then disappears to the background, accompanied by his followers. "That is one to one with the Resurrection liturgy in the Catholic Church for the Easter Vigil," Ludwig Mödl explains to me, when asked about Montgomery's criticism. He really cannot see the problem. "Of course, the Resurrection is indispensable as a historical event. But the form of representation is what's problematic. Do I present it boldly or in a way that comes closer to the historical event?" asks Mödl. "Historically, we only get to the edge of what happened there. We can say: Christ is risen and appeared. The only thing we know about the how, is that it was very quick and brief." He considers the guards to be dispensable. They are only there to prove that the body was not stolen.

In the end the scene was removed for staging reasons. Stückl was of the opinion that the Resurrection could not be depicted directly as a process. "'The Risen Lord has appeared' is what it says in all the Gospels," says Mödl. "There was a long discussion about what that might look like. But one thing is certain: he only appeared briefly. Even in the Baroque period, they reduced the striking representations somewhat. If you bring the risen Christ into the image, it does not correspond to the accounts of the appearance. You would no longer have that sense of the quick appearance. By making it fleeting, Stückl's portrayal comes much closer to the various descriptions." And to re-enact Jesus being bathed in a supernatural light on Mount Tabor as a voice from a cloud proclaims, "This is my beloved son", would probably be "somewhat bizarre to act out on stage."[64] And there were differences of opinion about whether you should actually take this miracle literally, as emerged when the delegation from Oberammergau visited the location itself in Israel in 2009. In any case, some people have a hard time with it.[65] And many Jews completely deny the Resurrection, Ludwig Mödl tells me: "It is said that it was an invention of the apostles, who had hallucinations. But this is interpreted in very different ways in Judaism, since every rabbinical school has a different interpretation. And they really do differ greatly, with some who say the literal opposite of others. All of this just stands side by side, they don't commit as firmly in Jewish theology as in Christianity."

There's always another Passion

In Oberammergau, theatre affects everyone. Scandal seems to arise here faster than anywhere else, because so much is at stake – tradition and belief and generally. Christian Stückl doesn't cause scandal for scandal's sake, he doesn't seek to provoke. But he wants to make theatre that he can stand behind. And if he can't do that without uproar, then so be it. He is at least as stubborn as his adversaries, after all. He touches on sore points, he argues rather than turning away when there's something at stake – and when it's the Passion at stake, he cares deeply. In the lead-up to the current Passion, he did not simply rely on the fact that his own position was secure. Instead, he stood for selection with his deputy director, Abdullah Kenan Karaca. "I wanted to spare Abdullah from having to go through this alone," he says. "That's why I said – we are a team." So a few of the votes didn't go his way, but somehow that is now part of the whole deal.

The answers Stückl came up with ten years ago are no longer valid today, or only of limited validity. "I'm far from finished with the Passion text," Stückl told me in autumn 2019. "The refugees, a different atmosphere for discussion – all of this feeds into the Passion." This time, too, there were conversations with Ludwig Mödl, but they were comparatively "short", as Mödl himself tells me. The problematic areas have been cleared up to the extent "that most of our Jewish partners are also satisfied. There will always be one or two who can still find something. But by and large the play has arrived in our times and it gives an appropriate form and a fine staging to the Jewish component of Christian history. Much finer, by the way, than the staging in some liturgies. It comes across as particularly strong and emotional. The prayer 'Shema Yisrael' before the Last Supper is the kind of scene you never forget."

But you never know what's coming with Stückl, he adds. "He is a bundle of ideas. He will call and say: 'I now have this idea and that, what do you think?' If I hesitate, he's on to the next idea. He is absolutely competent, in two respects: he knows the Bible and the numerous commentaries very well, and he is a gifted director – spontaneous, far-sighted and artistically ingenious." Mödl is still sceptical about the fact that the choir will no longer appear in liturgical costume – a reduction in solemnity he suspects will attract criticism. But he's willing to be surprised.

But the thing you always have to bear in mind is that the audience knows less and less about Christianity, so there are some things you need to clarify. Thankfully, Mödl adds with a laugh, it's rarely as bad as the Japanese journalist who came to Oberammergau in 2000: "She first went to Oberammergau for two days and afterwards to Füssen for the King Ludwig musical. She then wrote an article to say that there is a village in Europe where 2,000 people perform a play about a great guy who starts out as a social activist, then he's crucified and dies, then rises from the dead, but after a while drowns himself in Lake Starnberg because he's lovesick." The Ludwig musical as a continuation of the Passion, Jesus resurrected as the Bavarian fairy tale king. Things will never get that far in Oberammergau; the Stückl critics needn't worry.

MAKING-OF.
CROSSROADS ON THE PATH
TO THE PASSION

During the Passion, over 600 people are on stage at the same time in some scenes. The fact that all this usually happens with a fair degree of order is impressive enough in itself. That both the acting and the music are of such a high calibre that you sometimes forget you're watching amateurs is astonishing. Back in 2010 when I was watching the performance, I asked myself: how do they do it? How do they get so organised? And: where does this knowledge come from?

On music lessons and deficiency instruments

To be honest, in Oberammergau you basically never stop dealing with theatre and music. Preparations for the next Passion begin as soon as the previous one has come to an end. It starts with early musical education and promotion for the children. "The musical performance was long criticised as amateurish," Markus Zwink told me in October 2019 in the studio of the Passionstheater. "Franz Liszt, for example, could only stand to hear the first half of the performance when he visited in 1870." They would see which instruments were missing and find people to learn them. "Some people never played anything other than Passion music in their life," says Zwink. Unsurprisingly, the result was less than satisfactory. So gradually they began to invest in the musical education of the population. If you wanted to become a school teacher in Oberammergau you had to be musically proficient in singing, conducting or arranging. Ideally everything.

Today in Oberammergau there are two girls' and two boys' choirs, a youth and an adult choir, the local orchestra and a youth string orchestra, the "Nerven-Sägen". Instrument lessons are generously subsidised by the council. If a child takes it upon themselves to learn a so-called "deficiency instrument", such as oboe or bassoon, the council will even provide the instrument. The line-up of the Passion Orchestra is always in the back of your mind; learning to play an instrument is never just a hobby in Oberammergau. "The programme has been well received," says Zwink. "We also have regular musical events like carol singing, where the old musicians and choir singers always listen carefully. This means that children develop a feeling for quality from an early age."

But you can't completely avoid gaps. "We have plenty of women singing and a strong bass section. But like everywhere else, tenors are few and far between here, we simply don't have as many of them," explains Zwink. Overall, however, he is satisfied with the current state of things; there is a pool of 110 musicians, and there are always around 55 in the orchestra pit. The choir also has double the singers it needs. Of course, choirs and orchestras don't just rehearse in the Passion Year; the intervening years are years of practice.

Interludes

In 2005 Christian Stückl established interludes every summer in the Passionstheater, and since then theatre season in Oberammergau has never really stopped, even in the intervening years. They have performed "Jeremiah" by Stefan Zweig, an adaptation of Thomas Mann's novel "Joseph and His Brothers", as well as "A Midsummer Night's Dream" by William Shakespeare. As with

The musical education of future generations is a high priority for Markus Zwink.

the Passion, it is locals who take to the stage (although the performance right is extended to those not yet eligible to perform in the Passion). Some of them perform theatre almost every year. They are still amateurs, of course, but thoroughly trained. And over the years, Christian Stückl and deputy director Abdullah Kenan Karaca get to know their potential ensemble, which helps them later on as they cast the Passion Play. Rochus Rückel, for example, was part of the Passion 2010 as a child, and since 2012 he has regularly performed in the summer theatre: the nephew of Moses, a craftsman in "A Midsummer Night's Dream", in "Emperor and Galilean", "Geierwally", the title role in "William Tell" in 2018. More and more all the time. "I really enjoyed doing theatre," Rückel told me in the summer of 2021. "That was something that was really missing this year and last year during corona, it is sim-

The "performer selection" is an almost sacred moment in the village. Now the Passion season begins for everyone.

ply part of the village culture. You see each other in the theatre every evening, you don't even need a smartphone to meet up. A bit like the old days."

Through regular performances, Stückl gets to know his people, and after each Passion he is essentially keeping an eye out for the next. Who has what it takes to be Jesus? Who might be a compelling Judas? Where there were once "role dynasties" in the village (Stückl's family, for example, specialised in high priests), he wants to keep an eye on the next generation and promote new talent rather than old cronies. He needs 42 performers for the 21 leading roles, which are double-cast. Even if not everyone aspires to a speaking role and most are highly satisfied with a silent appearance in a crowd scene, 2,000 participants makes for a large pool from which to draw performers. Gigantic, even. Christian Stückl can't help looking out for talent, 24/7; in the pub, on the street, out shopping. For him, day-to-day life in the village is always one big audition, an ongoing casting round. He notes down who he intends to keep an eye on in his "little book". For example, he noticed Rochus Rückel years ago when Stückl gave a talk at his school. "He was only 14 and he just kept asking me questions," he remembers. "When something like that happens I write it down so I don't forget him." When Rückel took on ever larger roles in the intervening years, Stückl had already envisaged him as a potential Jesus long before 2018.

This pronounced concern for the next generation is a rather new development. Under the motto of "once a Jesus, always a Jesus", many performed for as long as they could. Whether the age of the performer more or less matched that of the role was secondary. And as women had to be under 35, Mary was not infrequently significantly younger than her son. When a generation of actors got too old, there was a lack of future performers. The decades-long insistence on the traditional and the brakes put on any attempts at reform meant young people were less and less inclined to perform in the second half of the 20th century. Before Stückl took over direction in 1990, the plays were a dusty, creaky affair. Something for fathers and grandfathers; for their critical and rebellious offspring it was more a target for boycott and revolt than a draw. Things are different today. Sophie Schuster, for example, is very clear that she wants to stay in "O'gau" – because of the Passion: "There are many people who study elsewhere, but everyone comes back here for the Passion. Because everyone wants to be part of it. It's just a lot of fun and it strengthens the team spirit. It's only every ten years, everyone wants to be part of it. Most of them keep their place of residence registered in

Oberammergau anyway when they go to university; the others move back in time to be able to participate."

This homecoming for the Passion was also a feature of earlier times. The attraction of acting together in theatre was always great, often greater than wanderlust. Anton Lang expressed this as early as 1930. And even if the essence is similar to what Sophie Schuster says today, he expresses it in far more dramatic terms: "What does Passion mean for the Oberammergau resident? Everything. He lives and dies for the Passion. [...] The Oberammergau resident always feels a secret longing, during the Passion Play he is driven homewards, especially the younger people who are away from home. Anyone who is prevented from attending by their studies, or anyone serving in the army or in a responsible position will complain: 'to be a child of Oberammergau and not be able to perform!' That's how it is for all who have to stay away."[66]

Preferred role: Romans

The concrete preparations for the Passion Play begin two years prior to the première, a good year before the rehearsals begin. All interested parties then have to submit an application form to the municipality, which is bureaucratically checked against the performance right. In this form you specify whether you have already performed, and in which part – with the option of stipulating your preferred role. It is actually rare for anyone to put "Jesus" in this category, says Christian Stückl. Most put nothing, but sometimes they request "Mary", "Judas" or even "director". It's usually in jest, but one applicant took against Stückl for interpreting his request for Pilate as a joke. "He left and never performed again," says Stückl. But a few have one wish: "Romans". The Roman soldier roles are particularly popular because they are exempt from the Hair and Beard Decree ... Some performers feign psoriasis as a medical reason for not being able grow hair under any circumstances (this is an argument among the singles, especially; evidently long beards don't go down that well with the ladies). Otherwise, applicants are asked to stipulate whether they can perform during the day or only in the evening, and how often they are available. There are around 110 performances each play year, with a mandatory minimum of 55 (before 2010 it was as many as 80). Anyone unable to put in the time is left out when it comes to assigning roles. Since 1980 only the 21 leading roles are double-cast, so all the others are replaced by someone else in an emergency.

All the application forms – around 2,000 in total – go to Christian Stückl. First he lets the fire commander pick his people, and Markus Zwink chooses the choir and orchestra. That still leaves 1,700. There are fifty fewer once the technical director has fished out his technicians. Now Stückl starts sorting into piles: "Number one might be for leads, number two for supporting actors, and then there are 'interesting people I haven't seen yet'. I'll audition them. Then I sort out the groups like the Romans and the mob, and at some point it becomes clearer and thinner." Until the very last day, who is playing whom shifts backwards and forwards; there are auditions in the Passionstheater which reveal whose voice carries to the back rows. Stückl explains to young people how to speak on a big stage so that you don't have to shout to be understood. It is also important to take a psychological approach, because "people get embarrassed in front of each other"[67] when it comes to speaking in the presence of their buddies in the group. A lead has to be able to work in a team, have the right voice and – subjectively – the right charisma, explains Stückl.[68]

Since 2010, Stückl has proposed a cast to the council which he "really puts to the test". He has sleepless nights before this date and "total panic". Because the municipal council has a veto right, even though it has never been exercised. Which is fortunate, because in 2010, for example, Stückl and his deputy director Otto Huber had three possible Christ candidates in their heads, two favourites. If the municipal council had rejected two, Stückl had nothing more up his sleeve.[69] In the past, the appointment process was much more complex; the council and the director would make suggestions. For example, out of eight possible Jesus actors, a first selection would produce a shortlist of three candidates. In 1990, Stückl went from one member of the council to another to persuade them to choose the person he wanted.

Performers avoid the hairdresser in the year before the première to ensure everyone has long hair and beards on stage.

Getting approval for Carsten Lück, the first Protestant in a leading role, was "really hard work", says Stückl. It was worth pushing for; after all, it was one of the few things that he could change back then, once his set design and his text reform had already been thrown out. There must have been turbulent scenes, with one or another faction storming out of the hall at times, and some wanted to reject Stückl's grandfather to get back at him. "Fortunately that didn't happen, otherwise I would have had trouble at home," he recalls. In 2000, Stückl introduced an open election by acclamation, which was essentially already anchored in the municipal code, and the new procedure in 2010. "It's much calmer now, people accept it much more readily than when it's a secret selection in the local council, where membership of a party or a club was often more important than the quality of the acting," says Stückl.

On 20 October 2018 the time had come: the day of the "performer selection". This is a ceremonial act in the village – and a sacred moment. This is the day that the Passion season officially begins. It starts with a procession from the Catholic to the Protestant church and on to the Passionstheater. There the Oberammergau residents come together in a ceremonial ecumenical service to renew the historic vow with which everything began almost 400 years ago. "In keeping with the vow and true to the promise of our ancestors, Oberammergau will perform the Passion Play in 2020" (the vow remains valid for 2022).

Then the lead actors of the Passion Play 2020 are announced in front of the Passionstheater. To make it more exciting (and because it is the tradition), their names are handwritten letter by letter in chalk on a huge blackboard. Next to "Judas", for example, appeared Cengiz Görür. He was just as astonished as his family and friends. Immediately this became the kind of minor sensation that the press tend to pounce on: the first Muslim in a leading role. Görür remained calm during the small "shitstorm" (a recent loan word in German) which ensued, a familiar response to any innovation in the traditional Passion Play.

For Sophie Schuster, the moment her name was written on the board was "somewhat surreal". Naturally it had crossed her mind that she'd like a speaking role. "But of course I also knew that there weren't many female roles. There are actually only six lead actresses. So I didn't really think I would get through," she says. "When my name went up, it was amazing. I was happy, but I also had a healthy respect for it. I had to let it sink in first. It took a few days before I truly realised what had happened."

The Hair and Beard Decree

On Ash Wednesday in the year before the Passion, the countdown to the première begins in a way that is visible to everyone in town: the "Hair and Beard Decree" calls on "all female and male participants and all children who take part in the Passion Play" to "let their hair grow, the men's beards too". No visit to the hairdresser from Ash Wednesday of the year prior to the Play until after the last performance in October of the following year. A hairy time in the village. The faces of the people of Oberammergau, especially the men, indicate how far away the première is. On Shrove Tuesday 2019, the hairdressers in the village were working flat out, with the last shave of the Jesus actors celebrated and recorded for eternity by local TV stations.

The day after the decree marks the beginning of a very quiet time for the hairdressers. Only those who aren't performing, the Romans and perhaps the odd person passing through come to have their hair cut, the others get a gentle beard trimming at most. However, when the Hair and Beard Decree had to be repeated in February 2021 due to the deferral to 2022, there were a few changes; the hairdressers were closed due to the corona lockdown, and many a performer's head had not seen scissors for a long time before this deadline.

The decree is a strange yet charming custom. "It's a very old tradition," explains Christian Stückl. "In the past only men were called upon to grow their hair and beards – women had long hair anyway – but now the decree applies equally to both sexes." Nobody can say for certain when exactly this rule was introduced. A poster with the decree has survived from 1950, but as far back as the Passion of 1870/71, photos show participants with long hair and beards. With the plays attaining global fame in the second half of the 19th century and the number of performances increasing, it was worth the effort of trying to look like the people of Israel might have looked: long hair, bearded.

The people on the stage were meant to make a homogeneous, historical and hairy impression. And when all the bearded men, young and old, stand in costume on the stage during the performances, it really does look impressive. Given the large number of participants, wigs and false beards are not an option. The decree is also intended to prevent brightly coloured hair or modern short hairstyles from disrupting the uniform look. Because naturally dyeing is also prohibited during this follicular Lent. But beyond that, letting your hair grow is a daily reminder of the common project, a community-building gesture and a token of humility, of sublimating your own needs to a higher goal.

The decree applies to everyone involved. From the mayor to the hotelier, from the student to the potter. The months of letting hair grow turn individuals into a community; it is a ritual approach to the play and to the role. "Normally you have a couple of hours in make-up to transform yourself into the character you are playing," says Andreas Richter, who played the role of Jesus in 2010 and will perform as Caiaphas in 2022. "But here you gradually become who you play over months. You look in the mirror every day, you see the change and you really grow into the role." Long hair can be a real problem, depending on the performer's profession. It is related that Josef Mayr, who played Christ in 1870, had to hide from his commander during his military service in the barracks because of his long hair and beard. And the Mayor of Oberammergau, Andreas Rödl, who was still in the police force when the 2019 decree was issued, had to apply to the Interior Ministry for special permission for his hairstyle. Because the normal rule for police is that hair must not reach or extend beyond the shirt collar. He got the permission. The reason given was the development of personal freedom, which weighed heavier than the uniform officer look.

Anyone who grows up in Oberammergau will inevitably have more intensive dealings with head and beard hair than the rest of the world. For boys especially, the Hair and Beard Decree demands a healthy level of self-confidence. Some of them tell me they are regularly mistaken for girls. Combine it with a sparse and somewhat uncool beard growth during puberty and you realise adolescents here don't have it easy. Andreas Richter knows that anyone between the ages of ten and twenty is caught in a difficult phase. "You are somewhere between childhood and adulthood. And then all of a sudden you have long hair and a few hairs on your face. Is anything growing there? How much? Do you really want something to grow there? It's a challenge that all Oberammergau males go through in their youth." At an age when you want to set yourself apart visually from others and, above all,

The ensemble at the Sea of Galilee in September 2019.

from your parents, something as personal as your hairstyle is suddenly determined from on high. "It must have been bad in 1968," says Christian Stückl. "The young hippies couldn't distinguish themselves from their parents with long hair. We've been a hippie village for 200 years."

There is one point of agreement: no one likes that in-between phase when hair is no longer short, but not yet long. When a man just looks like he's let himself go (even if that was a look that was widespread beyond Oberammergau in the time of corona and lockdown). "The rehearsals only start after the really bad time, your hair is quite long by then," says Andreas Richter. "But before that you see each other in town and think: 'He looks bad, is he sick?' Then you realise, 'no, he's just letting it grow'." Richter likes this time, when everyone changes externally, but also internally. "It's funny how a group of men will all start talking about hair and beard issues in rehearsals," he laughs. "Suddenly you see men with strange ribbons and headbands in their hair. Everyone tries to find an individual look, even though they basically look like everyone else." Head and facial hair may only be cut after the last performance.

And even if some find their long manes and shaggy beards annoying, as well as the impressive aesthetic, they bring people together. A problem shared is a problem halved. If one person isn't allowed to shave, he's a sad sap. If no one is allowed to shave, they become a community, and in this case: an ensemble.

Site meeting: Israel

In the September before each Passion, the core ensemble always comes together for the first time on a very special team education trip. Once again in 2019, for one week they travel to Israel, to the places said to have witnessed the historical Jesus and which have become part of the legend. All of the main actors and director Christian Stückl are on the trip. Musical director Markus Zwink also takes his music ensemble on a trip to Israel at the same time. Since Christian Stückl took over direction in 1990, this tour has become a tradition. Before that, there was collective religious instruction in the pub to get people in the mood – a rather dry affair. And one that barely inspired a wider focus. "Really unbearable theologians from Munich would come to our pub, sent by the bishop to on a 'people's mission'," Stückl tells me. "Everyone would sit there with their beers, listening to them talk about Judas' motivation and hoping that it would be over soon. That's how you really drive people away from religion." He spoke to Cardinal Wetter about his idea of replacing this teaching style with a trip to Israel. The Cardinal immediately offered his support. "It's just a different thing when you yourself stand in the village where everything started, where young men came together to change the world. It becomes a lot more vivid," says Stückl.

So now Israel. The beards and hair have now been growing for over half a year. The pictures and videos of the trip that I see show a rather peculiar group of pilgrims. In a café on the Via Dolorosa, the Way of the Cross in Jerusalem, Frederik Mayet filmed an everyday scene. As the bartender inside works the espresso machine, outside a small procession makes its way through the narrow alley from the old town to the Church of the Holy Sepulchre, the presumed site of the Crucifixion of Jesus. Five men and women carry, or rather drag a heavy wooden cross past the window, the others follow behind singing.

Mayet and the other leading actors mingled with all the believers, Christians, Jews and Muslims, who cohabit or coexist in this city. Here anyone can rent a cross or buy a crown of thorns for a few shekels and feel like Jesus for a day. And the theatre pilgrims also have an interest in tracing the story of Jesus which they will later stage together.

The Oberammergau group was housed in the Austrian pilgrims' hospice right on the Via Dolorosa. A plaque hanging on the wall commemorates the visit of the near-legendary Jesus actor Anton Lang, who made the pilgrimage here on his own in 1911. Photos show him with long hair and a beard in his pottery workshop and as Jesus in the play. Underneath is the note: "He portrayed Jesus three times in the Passion Play (1900, 1910 and 1922), achieving fame far beyond Europe. For example, the *New York Times* wrote in 1922 about the Passion Play and its leading actor Lang; but at the same time it mocked the Berlin government for doing too little to make this spectacle accessible to American tourists as well." The "Berlin government" may well have done that; unfortunately, we don't know who wrote the text on this plaque.

Inside the hospice you find Viennese café culture, outside falafel, pomegranates and hummus. Like a school trip, the programme included excursions and many conversations that brought the group closer together. Many of them didn't even know each other prior to the trip. The age difference between the youngest participant (16 years) and the oldest (78 years) was more than sixty years. "It's nice that different generations come together through the Passion and you get closer to people with whom you have little contact in everyday life," said Eva Reiser after the trip. Because of course there was also time for private exploration and the obligatory swim in the Dead Sea. And it really is a funny sight when you watch the film recordings of the trip from 2009: lots of bearded people, old and young, some with straw hats, others with a bottle of beer in hand, as they float about with Thomas Frauenlob from the Vatican Education Congregation. Sometimes they sat together in the evenings with a guitar and a beer, singing and talking about God, the world, everything.[70]

After the trip, everyone I spoke to was impressed. "It was never clear to me that Jesus and his disciples were deeply religious Jews," Rochus Rückel told me, for example. "They didn't set up a new religion, they tried to live their Jewish faith in its deepest form and to return to forgotten values." Seeing the scenes of the Passion through his own eyes, hiking through the steppe landscape of the Sea of Galilee, visiting the Church of the Holy Sepulchre and the Temple Mount – all this helps him get closer to his own portrayal of Jesus. "When I put my story together now, I have a real picture of the place in the back of my mind. I can imagine what it looked like back then," says Rückel. Mayet had a similar experience. Because even if a lot has changed in the past 2000 years, the distances are the same, the views from the Mount of Olives are similar. "When you know that, you go into the play with a different feeling," he believes.

As well as exploring the landscape and the original locations, Christian Stückl is always interested in the conflicts behind the story which have shaped its reception over the centuries: the confrontation with Judaism, the centuries-long dissemination of anti-Semitic messages through the Passion Play and their political appropriation in the Third Reich. That is why the tour group met with the Holocaust survivor Abba Naor. They talked about the Shoah, about faith and forgiveness. "I asked him if he still felt hatred," Mayet recalls. "He said no. He wants to break through the hatred, not pass it on to his children. You only have one life, he said, and life is a fine thing, so use it." A living example of the love for enemies that Jesus preached – the attempt to overcome hatred and enmity by renouncing vengeance. These encounters and the visits to the International Holocaust Memorial Yad Vashem left Stückl with no doubt: "Our mission as the German Passion Play is to remove such [anti-Semitic] things forever."[71]

Preparations in the background

The conceptual work on the Passion has long been at full speed when the ensemble travels to Israel. Since 2000, Stückl has formed part of a trinity of the Passion Play, an artistic triumvirate, with the musical director and composer Markus Zwink and the stage and costume designer Stefan Hageneier. All three share a determination to stay up to date in terms of aesthetics and content, to confront a changing world and its conflicts every ten years. Stückl works on the text, Hageneier on the aesthetics, Zwink on the music. It has long been a tradition to investigate the validity of the story for contemporary audiences. Stückl lets Jesus have more of a say, he wants to work out what Jesus was seeking, to show him as person of political convictions. He gives him more text to make his concerns clear, from the Sermon on the Mount for example. And Stückl doesn't want to portray Judas as just a one-dimensional traitor. He sees him as more complex, more like a friend who at some point rebels. "Jesus didn't choose someone who was just a bad guy from the start," says Stückl. "I would doubt Jesus in that case."[72] He doesn't want to reproduce stereotypes, rather he tasks the audience with confronting the questions that the team have been pondering for months.

Just fulfilling the vow and staging the Passion as a lucrative tourist spectacle – ultimately that's not the point. All three, Stückl, Hageneier and Zwink, have made art their profession beyond Oberammergau and the Passion Play. "Of course tackling the same story every ten years is unusual," Hageneier told me on my first visit. "But during this period you change, and of course so does the situation in which we live." This time, for example, the refugee issue will be reflected in the tableaux vivants, which embed the narrative in a larger context. "We are drawing the content of the tableaux vivants more closely together, as they fit together to form a continuous narrative of the displaced and oppressed Jewish people," says Hageneier.

While these images are designed in strong colours, he prefers "colourlessness" for the play scenes. "Here I have a stage 45 metres wide and a large auditorium. I need a long-range effect," he explains. "We also perform mostly in daylight, with no lighting. The crowd has to be integrated into the set and optically recede into the background to bring the main characters to the fore." So the basic colour of the set is also the basic colour of the costumes for the crowd. Hageneier resumed contact with his fabric suppliers in India, sent them beige-grey colour samples of the set and sketches for samples – and commissioned thousands of metres of specially dyed fabric. These are combined with old fabrics. "A real silver brocade fabric simply has a completely different effect on the stage than a dyed one," says Hageneier. But he always sticks to a historical aesthetic. It is not the ambition of the Passion Play to transfer what is happening to today. "We don't want to turn it into contemporary theatre and portray the Romans as Nazis," says Hageneier. "They simply stand for a military power, for a force. So how do you represent that? We have to show them in a way they might plausibly have looked. The challenge is that you don't make them look too much like the Romans in 'Asterix and Obelix', so they become comical characters."

It takes incredibly intense preparation to ready the props for the five-hour performance. Every ten years they allow for greater effort here than would be conceivable elsewhere. Not just with the wings with their thousands of feathers. Each new production requires new crosses made of solid wood, because safety concerns dictate that the previous models, subjected to stress ten years prior, cannot be used. After all, the feet of Jesus hang three metres above the stage. The fittings for all the tableaux vivants have to be made, half a village has to be dressed for the collective play. The performers are measured, their costumes are sewn and tried on. At the beginning of the season, the choir and the crowd renew the vow of 1633 – in historical costumes. That means another set of completely new costumes. Nine cubic metres of styrofoam are transformed into an impressive Golden Calf in 300 hours of sculpture and 180 hours of painting. For each performance,

Stefan Hageneier redesigned the stage building for the current play.

Barbara Lampe makes a huge clay jug in her pottery, which Jesus will smash on the floor in the merchants' scene in the temple.

Where it all happens

When I visited the Passionstheater with Stefan Hageneier in 2019, the main stage was under scaffolding. Workers were busy bricklaying, plastering, painting. It was almost nothing like normal theatre construction. Brick walls instead of plywood backdrops, house paint rather than scrims. Certainly, when I walked around the stage and through the workshops, it was more a breath of eternity than the ephemeral nature of the theatre that I experienced. And one year later, in October 2020, the building actually received a kind of eternal seal of approval: the Passionstheater was placed under a preservation order. "The building is worthy of protection due to its special construction and design, the rare technology in the stage and its high historical significance for the popular and amateur theatre," said the press release of the Bavarian State Office for Monument Preservation. And: "With the Oberammergau Passion Play already a UNESCO Intangible Cultural Heritage site, the registration of the theatre building in the list of monuments now also pays tribute to its structural and material heritage."

The building is now under monument protection in its current state. This probably also includes the stage design by Stefan Hageneier. Well, it's not an ordinary, mobile stage set like you'd find in a normal theatre, it's not a mock-up, it's solidly bricked and plastered. Nevertheless, this is a rare, if not unique, accolade for a set designer. Because for the first time in a long time, the stage for the 2020/22 play was really worked over, which means not just painted, but truly transformed in form and design. "Stefan Hageneier wanted to bring in more even, steadier lines," Carsten Lück explained to me as I once again walked through the theatre with him to hear about the structural details. Once round, the arches were replaced with straight ends, and everything was covered with grey mineral plaster. Before that, the stage set from 1930 had been used for decades. In future, any construction work must be agreed with the monument protection authority. "That makes it a little more complicated," says Lück, "but it does not mean that there will be no more changes." And he stresses that they always carried out previous changes with great diligence. "We have always been careful to proceed as discreetly as possible."

In the Passionstheater, everything is designed for the particular – and changing – requirements of the play. The people of Oberammergau have always been creative when it comes to making the necessary and desired possible. There are a few things you don't normally find in a theatre, such as the "donkey ramp" which allows the theatre animals an easy entrance onto the stage. And the entrance has been enlarged upwards as well to ensure the camels don't hit their heads. The iron curtain which separates the stage and auditorium as a fire protection measure opens up and down like a fish's mouth. It can't be simply pulled up because there is no flyloft. Space behind the stage is scarce in any case, with everything strictly organised according to logic and sequence. For example, because the choir appears so often, the choir dressing room is closest to the stage. The crowd have to move in stages because there is not enough space in the dressing room for everyone at the same time. It is a major logistical effort to get the increasing number of participants on and off the stage without bottlenecks.

The theatre in its current form is much more recent than the play itself. In 1830 the play was relocated to the Passionswiese, a field in the north of the village. King Ludwig I only allowed it to be held on the condition that it would no longer take place in the cemetery (which was likely to have been quite devastated after performances). The spectators initially sat on wooden stands, mostly outdoors – only the boxes were covered. Sometimes it was a little risky, as Burton describes – with slight exaggeration, as usual: "Amongst the rough Northern peasants who compose 'Das Publikum', an opened umbrella or a parasol would at once be clubbed down; men and women defend their heads with broad-brims, shawls, or as they best can. [...] The platform is well put up, but the weight makes it shaky, unpleasantly affecting the nervous, and suggesting ugly contingencies."[73] Fortunately, these "ugly contingencies" did not come to pass; the temporary building didn't collapse, nor was there a mass panic.

In 1899, the Munich court theatre engineer Max Schmucker designed a permanent auditorium that was built on the Passionswiese. "The seats rise toward the back so that the foothills of our Bavarian Alps form part of the play for the higher seats, creating

When the main rehearsals begin in the Passion Play, the stage fills up and the director has to sort the crowd.

a wonderful natural backdrop," wrote Anton Lang.[74] Above the grandstand is a filigree scaffolding structure with six steel arches on which the wooden hall rests: today's Passionstheater, which is open at the front facing the open-air stage.

So since the beginning of the 20th century, rehearsals and performances have taken place in a permanent theatre building in the north of the village centre. Since its inauguration, this theatre has been in a constant process of further development. Its story is a story of rebuilding. Every ten years it was brought up to date with the latest technology and adapted to the needs of the times. In 1922, for example, a photo studio was added to the rear of the dressing room building, which is now used for meetings and as the creative headquarters. In 1980, a huge lifting platform was built at the back of the stage for a special effect, which appeared out of nowhere in the Mount of Olives scene. As it has not been used since then and was taking up a lot of much-needed space, it was removed again for the current Passion. In 2010 lighting bridges were added, as lights were required once the play was transferred to the evening.

A mobile roof was also designed to move over the stage if necessary to protect against rain, snow or even hail. In 2019, sound insulation was added to the rear auditorium to support the new electro-acoustic sound system. All of this in response to one question: how can we do it just a little bit better?

Rehearsal period

It started in December 2019. After an initial reading, Stückl rehearses on a small scale with his main ensemble, Zwink with the choir, orchestra and soloists. On evenings during the week, and on the weekends. Stückl works with his actors on the tempo and intonation, demonstrates how phrases are to be declaimed, works through their meaning, the concerns and emotional states behind the words. Where is the emphasis? What is important here? What does the character want to say? Word for word, he works his way through the text with each of the actors.

As rehearsals begin, hobbies, leisure and the rest of village life fall away. "You don't see your friends as much, you don't go on holiday …" Frederik Mayet tells me. "There is a rehearsal almost every evening and at the weekend." It's often a lot, actually it's too much at times if you are also doing your job on the side. "But you can't beat yourself up, you do what you can and do it as well as possible. And if you have to drop something, you just have to deal with it," says Mayet. Things have changed since 2010; he is now married and has two children. "So the question is: can I really do it all? Of course it is exhausting, but it is only every ten years." Andreas Richter also confirms that the Passion saps your strength: "The role of Jesus requires a huge amount of commitment. My family had to put up with a lot," he said in a podcast in 2021. "We were also expected not to do anything risky or that might result in broken bones. I like to ski and go to the bike park, which was a bit difficult for me to give up for a year."[75]

It is helpful if your employer at least recognises the importance of the play and doesn't stand in the way. "During this time your capacity is not the highest, you have to reduce your working hours. That is quite demanding, you have a full-time job on the side," says Richter. During the Passion 2000 he was studying in Regensburg, and the student chancellery did not allow him a semester off, even though he presented signatures from the district administrator and the director. Now he is active in the social field; his commitment is recognised there, it has a higher priority.

In late January 2020 the whole thing heads to the main stage. It is cold. And it's full. Hundreds of people press into the Passionstheater for the first rehearsal of the crowd. The cold has always been part of it. "As soon as the weather permits, the rehearsals take place outdoors, and even hands and noses frozen blue don't deter people from participating," said Anton Lang in 1930. "One Thomas even gave his life shortly before the start of the play due to pneumonia that he contracted during rehearsals."[76] It rarely comes to such a dramatic end; it may be uncomfortable today, but it's bearable.

Everyone comes to this very special village meeting: the old, the young, women, men, mothers, fathers, children and grandchildren, the snowboarders, the students, the wood carvers and the mountain rescue teams. The thing they have in common is their desire to take part in the Passion Play – and their long hair and beards. The audience seating is still covered, the stage is empty. A few rays of sun struggle past the retractable roof. Around the edge are the stagehands' tools, the prepared column capitals.

Director Christian Stückl is standing on a long table by the ramp, facing the stage, a microphone in his hand. It's important that everyone can see and hear him. All participants have to check in with their chip cards at the entrance; the number of participants makes an individual roll call impossible. Once the escape routes and fire protection regulations have been explained, they're ready to start. On the agenda today are the "Outrage" and the "Way of the Cross". During the "Outrage" 457 extras from the crowd are on the stage, plus around 200 players: leading actors, High Councillors, Romans including flagellants, the servants of Pilate and Caiaphas as well as poor people. It's the biggest scene. So Stückl sorts the masses: he sends the Romans downstage and the crowd, who are divided into four groups, into different areas of the stage. There is one leader per section of the crowd who was present at the first rehearsals in the small theatre to represent their group. They are briefed in advance by the director and can later pass on the exact sequence to their group. Before the major stage rehearsals, they are assigned other actors from the crowd who are familiar with all the cues. When everyone comes together in January, at least some of them will already know where to go on stage.

Here and now it's about the fundamentals: who comes from which part of the wings? Who calls what when? Where moments ago everybody was just running around in chaos and it was hard to imagine all these people even fitting on the stage, everyone finds their place surprisingly quickly. "Let the Nazarene die!" they shout in unison. "Die!" When so many people in the choir call for the death of an individual, it can't fail to make an impact. From one moment to the next, the initial chaos has given way to a concentrated and threatening mood. There it is, the tumultuous, whipped-up mob. The Crucifixion is about to begin. The ski suits are forgotten.

Despite the cold it feels a bit like Jerusalem. "That sounds pretty good!" says Stückl and explains the situation: "During these last shouts, the whole of Rome rumbles in! If you're heavy on your feet, please stand at the edge. I want to really see something happening!" Caution is a priority when so many people have to move around a confined space. Especially since quite a few are "heavy on their feet", as Stückl calls it. There is also a step in the wings that "wasn't there before". Before – that is, ten years ago, with the last Passion.

You can tell that Stückl, who is in charge of the play for the fourth time, has experience. He is not perturbed by the masses of people, his euphoria is contagious. He warns the Romans that

The first rehearsal of the Crucifixion in 2020: Christian Stückl breaks it down for Rochus Rückel.

their lances are pointed ("genuine", as Hageneier would say). They don't want any injuries, so the tips have to stay upright. Stückl runs back and forth, he's long since abandoned his woollen jacket, he's the only one who's warm on the frosty, draughty open-air stage. He plays all the roles, directs and motivates the crowd. "Now the High Council comes out of the middle, you mingle with members of the crowd nearby," he shouts. "On your marks, get set, go!" And there it is, tumult on the stage. Bigger than any other theatre.

The rehearsal is an event in the village. Local non-performers, neighbours and children, but also tourists just passing through find their way to the open Passionstheater. At the end, the two Jesus actors are standing in the centre of the stage, where the Cross will later be placed. Even if it is just a simple wooden slat today. And even if they don't hang, but simply hold them, there is an inkling of what it will be like one day. "He's about to hang!" shouts Stückl, inimitably conveying the mood among the people, the excitement. And the pain.

The Crucifixion

The highlight and the greatest technical challenge of the play is of course the Crucifixion. Indeed, the scene even aroused something like awe from Richard Burton. He called it the "gem of the piece"; however his translator Susan Urban used the Bavarian term "Schmankerl" (a word more often used to a describe tasty treat), which seems a little strange in this context. "Two crosses are seen at the Podium as the curtain rises; the thieves, with bare heads and wild hair, hang on by their arms being passed over the cross-piece. The central Cross, slowly raised from the ground by the hangman, drops into its socket, and the tall white figure, apparently only nailed on, hangs before us."[77]

As this report shows, the Crucifixion was only partially visible to the public up to and including 1990. The Cross was carried across the stage, then came a tableau vivant. In the summer of 2021, on the terrace of the theatre café Stückl walked me through how it went. "You could hear the hammer blows and the melodramatic singing: 'I can hear your limbs ache as they are pulled out of their joints,' it started. Then the violins played. 'Whose heart would not quake when he hears the hammer's blow?' The horns played." When the curtain rose again, the crosses and the victims were on the stage and facing the audience. But Stückl wanted less pathos, and instead to show what really happened: the brutality of this process, which is not necessarily apparent when you see a relatively calm and dignified Jesus hanging on the Cross.

So he changed the process; since 2000 the entire Crucifixion has taken place on the open stage. Incidentally, this was an idea that Schwaighofer had already experimented with in the Rosner rehearsal. And there was something else that Stückl changed. While visual depictions often show only Jesus nailed to the cross, with the two thieves to the left and right of him tied, he wanted three crosses of the same size and three equal crucifixions with nails. The pastor objected, pointing out that tradition dictates that Jesus dies on the Cross and suffers more than the others. Stückl, who knew how to argue by now, replied with the Bible; there is no evidence that Jesus was treated differently than the two robbers who were crucified with him. "The two criminals were crucified exactly as Christ was, one hundred percent. There are a few theologians who doubt it, but nobody takes them seriously today," confirms Ludwig Mödl. "In the late Gothic period, people began to portray the other two as tied to emphasise the contrast with Christ. These are psychological elements which have prevailed in iconography, but are not historical." The Passion pays attention to correctness elsewhere; in Oberammergau, for example, the Crucifixion nails are not struck through the palms of the hands (as is often falsely portrayed in visual depictions), but (seemingly) through the carpal bones.

The challenge was and is to stage this complex process so skilfully that it looks real from the front row. When the Jesus actor has placed the Cross on the stage, the executioners put him on his back. The climbing harness hidden under his loin cloth is inconspicuously attached to the Cross. He can put his feet on a tiny step, he puts his hands on the "nails" which are hooked into the wood and arch invisibly around the wrist. Then the executioners pull the recumbent Cross from the front with ropes into a vertical position, with pushing from behind. Like a maypole, the Cross is wedged into a recess in the ground. – "This is a very important moment, for me as well," says Frederik Mayet. "When you hear these hammer blows and the Cross is erected, it is so powerful. You get a completely different feeling for what is going on; it's a brutal murder." To ensure that everything goes smoothly, there is extensive rehearsal. First the two Jesus characters are measured and their crosses adjusted to their individual proportions. Then there is a technical "hanging rehearsal" in which the Cross is set up with the actor for the first time. Vertigo can be an issue; the Crosses are 5.45 metres high, with Christ's feet hanging about three metres above the stage. Frederik Mayet remembers his first time in 2010 well. "When the Cross went up, I had the feeling that I was falling over because the Cross was swinging," he tells me. "Then it became crystal clear

It takes a certain degree of trust to submit yourself to this procedure. The actor playing Jesus can't be afraid of heights either.

to me: now you are really playing this role, now you really are Jesus in the Passion." Rochus Rückel also had the feeling during the first hanging rehearsal that this would be "the strangest moment in the Passion play". Even if he was in a great mood and one of the executioners was a good friend of his; even though they were "not yet so advanced", not yet "emotional": "You become aware that you are performing death, and in such an exposed position, in which you have relatively little room to manoeuvre. Half-naked three metres above the stage, that's quite scary."

In the course of rehearsals everyone grows into their roles and becomes more confident. At some point they take off their bobble hats and put on their costumes, a month before the première there are entire run-throughs. And then there are always those moments when Christian Stückl is gripped by a shudder. "Suddenly you ask yourself: how did he manage it? When you're aware, when it really hits home and it suddenly takes on a different level." In the lead-up year, the ensemble approaches the Passion step by step as if on a Way of the Cross over the same stations of the Crucifixion of Christ, which they ultimately act out over a hundred times in their theatre, one summer long. Rituals, some of them centuries old, and a thoroughly (self-)critical view of one's own history blend into a store of experiences, with which they repeatedly examine the story of the Passion. The young actors alone ensure that the production is not a copy of the previous one. The ten-year break also ensures that Stückl and his team start over every time. In ten years the world changes and people with it. In ten years people marry and have children. In ten years, people die. In ten years everyone will get a lot older. Anyone who was a child last time is an adult this time. Or as the director puts it: "It's the same story, but it's always different."

JESUS CHRIST SUPERSTAR.
PLAYING THE LEAD

Even if this theatrical event is collective, there is of course one role that is the centre of attention. In the village and in the auditorium. Jesus. His Crucifixion is the climax of the Passion, its reason for existence. There are actually few other plays that are so focused on one scene, this indisputable climax that everything comes down to, "The Oberammergau Play of the Passion of Jesus of Nazareth", to use the title of the 2010 text. Everyone knows the story and its outcome – and yet: "When you are up there hanging on the Cross, you feel how people suffer. Although everyone knows what is going to happen, everyone seems to hope that things won't get that far," says Frederik Mayet, recalling his depiction of Jesus. When the blows of the hammers on the massive wooden cross boom throughout the theatre, it is a

What else does Jesus have to say to us today? It's a question which preoccupies Frederik Mayet.

shocking moment – not only for believers. Even the perpetually niggling Richard Burton could not avoid words like "magic" and "overwhelmed" in describing this scene: "We have seen them in thousands, artistic and inartistic; but we never yet felt the reality of a man upon a cross. The glamour of the legend is over us; and we look upon, for the first time, what we shall not forget to the last."[78]

The overwhelming feeling that the audience feels at this moment is of course transferred to the Jesus performers. Frederik Mayet still remembers his first Crucifixion before an audience in 2010: "It really does something to you," he tells me. "You hang there, half-naked, exposed, being mocked and evaluated. It's just pretty uncomfortable, you feel the audience's horror, it's an extreme situation." And even if everything is, of course, just theatre: "You feel what the crucified feel, you think how cruel it must have been to spend hours or days there." When Jesus then speaks his last words, there is an "indescribable calm" in the auditorium: "Normally you always hear a cough or something, but then suddenly it is as quiet as a mouse."

For the audience, the Crucifixion is the most moving scene in the play, for the Jesus actors it is the most exhausting. It is a moment of utmost responsibility. Quite a few audience members begin to cry, others are sunk in prayer. The Jesus character attracts one hundred percent of the attention, while the actor has to struggle with all sorts of adversities. It can be bitingly cold, but that is the least of the problems; at least, it didn't bother Mayet, with all the adrenaline he felt at that moment. Rochus Rückel, who has previously only hung on the Cross as a test, describes how everything up there wobbles terribly when you move. To portray Jesus you certainly need to be free of vertigo. There are no real accidents recorded, but there have been some dangerous situations. In his memoirs, Anton Lang describes how they failed to attach the Cross properly during a performance in 1910. "[Once] the nail that held the Cross to the ground was accidentally misplaced; they had to raise the Cross by crudely fastening it with chains. That day I felt it must be my last play; because if the Cross had fallen with me, I would have lain shattered beneath it."[79]

Fortunately, there have been no such accidents so far. From one Jesus generation to the next, the performers pass on behavioural tips that make the time on the Cross more bearable. For example, if you sneeze "when you are already dead", tickle the top of your palate with your tongue and the sneezing reflex will disappear, as Frederik Mayet learned from Anton Burkhart, who played Jesus in 2000. It is also not a good idea to eat cake in the cloakroom beforehand; the aromas and crumbs caught in your beard attract wasps and bees. If they're circling around your mouth when you're hanging on the Cross, things can get uncomfortable. Keeping your arms in place for twenty minutes is also a challenge. They tend to go to asleep when they hang in the metal nail loops for so long and run the risk of slipping down. But it does help to clench your hands into a fist as long as you can while Jesus is still alive.

Selecting Jesus

While all the other participants only find out what role they have been assigned on the day of the performer selection, the two Jesus actors are warned by Christian Stückl the evening before. Frederik Mayet still remembers Stückl calling him in 2010 after the council meeting. In 2000 he played John and was very close to the two Jesus actors. "They were such role models for me, I would never have imagined I could do it," he says. "It was almost too sacred for me. But because I had such great confidence in Christian, I realised he knows what he's doing." The first days and weeks he was still "quite overwhelmed". "I went through the village without looking at anyone and thought to myself, 'Oh God, now everyone knows you.' You are really known in the village from one day to the next and you are totally in focus. You also notice what kind of responsibility that brings, that it is important to everyone here." He put himself under pressure and it took a while to become really free. The ambition to do well was enormous. After a few Jesus film evenings including Monty Python, Mel Gibson and Pier Paolo Pasolini, he realised that everything is interpretation, that he had to find his own way. This time he can take a much more relaxed approach to the task; after all, it worked well last time.

Rochus Rückel already had an inkling when Stückl asked him to make himself available the evening before the performer selection. "But actually you don't even dare to think that because you think it's presumptuous. You don't want to think of yourself as something better or disregard others," he says with his signature modesty. In the evening he was with his best friend and their girlfriends when the call came and Stückl asked him to come over again. "Then he told me and I was amazed. You know it, but you haven't internalised it," he says. He then tricked his friends into believing he was Judas. After all, he wasn't allowed to reveal anything before the official performer selection.

For him, the highlight of the rehearsals was driving out the merchants with the entire crowd. "I really had a sense of, that's how it is now, you are playing Jesus," he says. "I still remember how in 2010, as children we always waited before the Entry into Jerusalem for Frederik or Andreas [Richter] to come with his

Rochus Rückel performs the part in the knowledge of being part of something bigger. His humility keeps him grounded.

apostles. And I thought how crazy it is that he is playing Jesus," he says. Now he is the one who will ride the donkey to change the world.

Who is this Jesus? What distinguishes him? How did he live? These are the questions that have been preoccupying Christian Stückl since he staged the Passion. He wants to show him as someone who poses questions of society, as an irritant and perhaps also as a provocateur. When Stückl started out, still young and wild himself, he saw Jesus as a "loud revolutionary"[80]. He now sees him primarily as a challenge. One who will not accept others being oppressed, or interactions and language becoming brutalised. "Jesus is an imposition," said Stückl in an interview in 2018, "because he demands things from me that I would not be able to achieve in my own life. I can't even describe what he is like, just what I can feel, what his life demands of us. We have been living with Christianity for 2000 years, but nobody is really ready to live what he demonstrated to the utmost."[81]

I've thought more about Jesus in the last two years than I have in my entire life before. I have found that this figure (because I personally still find it difficult to imagine him as a real historical person) has much more to offer than death on the Cross, which is so omnipresent. I also took a look at the Jesus films by Monty Python, Pier Paolo Pasolini, Mel Gibson and, most recently, Milo Rau. In December 2020 I talked to Frederik Mayet about Rau's film "The New Gospel". He didn't find it a bit surprising that Rau transfers the plot to Italian refugee camps. "Jesus was someone who went to the margins of society and surrounded himself with outcasts, whores and the sick," he said. "He was someone who saw grievances, went and tried to make things better. If you look at the Matera region now, where refugees live under precarious circumstances and women have to prostitute themselves, where people are exploited and treated badly by the authorities – then of course that is a consistent analogy to history 2000 years ago." It is this view, which draws an arc from then to now, which makes studying Jesus worthwhile for those who are not believers or who are not Christian. And which makes the story of this person relevant to this day. Or, as Andreas Richter puts it: "This Jesus is a person who is courageous and consistently goes his own way, not deviating a millimetre from his values. Christian Stückl works through how he struggles with it, how anger and fear germinate in him, but he transcends it again, if you will. You can learn a lot from this because we chase after our feelings and needs all day like simple mammals."[82]

The question of what Jesus still has to say to us today is inevitably followed by many others. How do you deal with refugees and global inequality? How do you live in a world where there are so many poor people and so much wealth concentrated among so few? Mayet is convinced that you need this social urgency to tell the story today. "This 'if you don't fight for yourselves, nobody will fight for you'."

The focus is on whoever is playing Jesus, which some people feel as a burden as well as a great honour. Before the double cast for all leading roles was introduced in 1980, the identification of the person with the role was even greater than it is today. When the actors for the Passion in 1960 were announced in 1959, a documentary by the Bavarian state broadcaster announced: "The Preisinger Anton is re-selected. Another difficult year is approaching for the 47-year-old hotel owner […]. Of course he is pleased that he is allowed to play this important role for the second time. […] But when the autograph hunters and hand-shakers from all over the world harass him from morning to night, then he will sometimes sneak out of the house to be alone for a few hours, like he did ten years ago."[83] Anton Preisinger is seen as something like the first pop star among the Oberammergau actors; it is said that his wife had to bring his food to the theatre, otherwise he would have been knocked over by the crowds. "In 1960, Anton Preisinger will be just as famous as Curd Jürgens or Marlon Brando," they claimed in the aforementioned documentary.[84]

Even if that seems exaggerated, there is still a lot of attention today. As a Jesus actor, you are a focus of interest and the public from one day to the next, giving interviews and appearing on TV talk shows. For Rochus Rückel it was particularly strange, because the postponement of the Passion from 2020 to 2022 extended the advance attention by two years. In the summer of 2021 he told me: "I've been in the public eye for almost three years now, although I haven't done anything yet. It's a bit strange." He also noticed that after he was selected, he was contacted by many people who didn't necessarily feel the need to talk to him beforehand. Frederik Mayet had some strange encounters with fanatical fans in 2010. A woman from Ohlstadt posed as a journalist and interviewed him. But when she made a pass at him with increasing insistence, he broke off the conversation. Another time he came home and found a cake with a letter on the table – from an "older guy from Murnau" who had just walked into his living room. Mayet called him and confronted him, but the man didn't understand the fuss; after all, the door wasn't locked. Mayet also received a lot of fan mail at the time. "Most of the encounters were very nice," he tells me. For example, when people who had seen him play the day before engaged him in conversation. Or when Chancellor Angela Merkel watched the play and visited him for a chat in the dressing room. "When I got changed afterwards and I was standing there in my underpants, she came in again and said, really cool: 'Don't worry about me, keep changing, I won't look, I just have to make a short phone call.' She still had to give a statement about the unemployment figures, she couldn't ever relax. It was very funny," Mayet recalls.

Role versus performer

In 2010 Ulrike Bubenzer saw an American lady rush into the museum and scream: "I saw Jesus on a bike!" Sometimes the role and the actor merge in people's perceptions. "For her it was Jesus on the bike, she was completely blown away," says Bubenzer. "In this respect, the double casting is good, because if you have to take it on alone, it's almost too much for one person." There are stories in the village that some of the Jesus actors never managed to resume normal life. These myths, which some credit and others vehemently deny, revolve primarily around one person: Anton Lang, who played Jesus in 1900, 1910 and 1922. According to the story, even between Passions he kept his hair long, minted coins with his likeness as Jesus on them and years later went through the village blessing people. Was that really the case? His granddaughter Monika Lang can't bear to hear these stories any more: "None of the people I spoke to and who knew him confirmed that," she tells me.

In his autobiography he comes across as a godly and humble man: "The role of Christ demands multiple forms of renunciation from its bearer. Great is the responsibility of those who are to live up to what they will never reach."[85] He even expressly describes that it was others who "could not distinguish between actors and characters". For example, the French marquise who wrote to tell him that he "must not marry because Christ was not married either" or "the mother who brought her child after a performance" so that he would bless them.[86] He describes his play as "worship; fulfilment of a high mission, the highest mission"[87]. Only in the captions does he sometimes mix up roles and people, for example where it says "Peter, Judas and I reading a letter from home" or "Peter after skiing"[88].

So it is impossible to conclusively determine whether the stories are just rumours or not. But their mere existence confirms one thing beyond all doubt: the great importance attached to the Jesus actor. Not only was Lang received by the Pope, his family benefited from his fame even after his death. When the Americans marched into Oberammergau after the Second World War, the commandant placed the Langs' pension under protection because he had lived here in the "House of Jesus" as a child, Monika Lang tells me. "Nobody was billeted with us and we didn't have to leave."

Even if the identification with the role was probably different in the past and neither Mayet nor Rückel is in danger of floating away, Frederik Mayet believes that this role has changed him. "It does something to you," he told me in 2020 during a conversation in the garden of the Münchner Volkstheater. "I think differently about religion. That it should be something that integrates, where you include people. The Church is often very far removed from its core message. It's not that I've become a better person now, but I might listen a little more to my inner compass and try to take a stand, a position."

The change that Mayet describes is an alignment with his values, the pursuit of greater coexistence. Richter also sees a lot in the figure that has application in everyday life. "When it comes to

In the Romans' dressing room in 2010. When you have a lot of people performing together you can expect horseplay.

charity, dealing with conflicts, in your own family, with your own children, you keep coming back to the message of Jesus; fighting back doesn't help. The question, 'Why doesn't he defend himself?' is of great interest to children, it is very close to the reality of their lives."[89] The confrontation with Jesus forced the two Jesus actors from 2010 to ask themselves fundamental questions anew. Yet there is no sign that either lost their grip on reality. Rochus Rückel, who is so far a Jesus in waiting, carries himself with great modesty, which is not a lack of self-confidence, but rather the awareness of being part of something larger. "Certainly, something has changed," he told me in the summer of 2021. "This is the number one topic among all my friends at uni in Munich, my family, friends of my parents. Of course having a Jesus in your family is something special. But I always thought it was a role, that's why it hasn't made me more Christian."

BACKSTAGE.
TURMOIL IN THE WINGS

Viewed from the auditorium, the Passion Play is an over-whelming theatrical spectacle, which, given the numerous contingencies, (mostly) takes place with an almost un-canny perfection. Certainly at the 2010 première, despite all the adults, children, animals and technical challenges, nothing went wrong (at least nothing that I noticed). But the theatre that goes on behind the scenes is different: the word *Schabernack* (practical joke) comes up in conversation with remarkable frequency among all participants. Some are amused, others (Christian Stückl) less so. And the children, it must be said, are generally less inclined to jest than the grown-ups.

In the case of the tableaux vivants, bystanders often stand in the wings trying to get a laugh out of the performers, who have to remain silent in their positions. Ink is sometimes mixed into Pilate's water so when he washes his hands they come out blue, or spirits are poured into the communion wine. "There's a lot of nonsense which goes on," Christian Stückl tells me. "Once they stuck a naked woman over the text on the roll with the death sentence. It emerged that the lad who had to proclaim it had never learned the text by heart, but always read it. You don't even notice it when you rehearse. He was so shocked, he just stammered: 'Is condemned.' Actually, they are reliable, but sometimes they just get carried away. During the performance I'm always busy just making sure that everyone stays where they were."

The "catalogue of sins"

All sorts of customs have developed over the decades or centuries which are intended to hold the team together and keep it in line. Every dressing room has its own rules, some even draw up a "catalogue of sins". "The apostles are particularly keen," Frederik Mayet tells me. "Anyone who laughs or grins on stage has to pay five euros. Being absent without excuse at the apostle barbecue costs twenty euros." Other "sins" that attract punishment: arriving too late for the rehearsal, missing the performance, a costume error like forgetting the prayer shawl, when a Roman drops his spear … In every dressing room there is a cash box where the fines are collected. At the end of the day, they use it to buy snacks or make a donation. "Of course, it helps ensure discipline. It doesn't hurt that everyone is keeping an eye on things and that they maintain morale even after the seventieth performance," says Mayet. That's because: "Nonsense on stage is punished severely." (Anyone who has a birthday on a performance day has to buy a round of snacks in the dressing room, even if they haven't sinned beforehand.) Well, you might think, they seem to regulate themselves. Christian Stückl sees it a little differently. When I mention the "catalogue of sins" in our conversation, he groans: "That is the worst thing of all. If you have to pay a fine of ten euros for laughing on stage, it tempts some to make others laugh. Then you're just provoking mistakes. I would like to forbid these catalogues of punishments altogether."

But on the day of the première, at least, proceedings are conducted with great solemnity, there is no sign of the coming nonsense. In the morning, much like the day of the performer selection, the musicians process from the Catholic to the Protestant church and finally to the Passionstheater, where the season begins with an ecumenical service. After lunch with guests of honour from the political and ecclesiastical spheres, the play begins in the early afternoon. "There is such a spirit of optimism", Monika Lang tells me enthusiastically. "It's finally under way. You are motivated and excited and everyone hopes that we will do well and that nothing bad happens. It really hits you, after rehearsing for months when you come in from the wings and see the theatre full of people. I always have tears in my eyes." Which half of the pairs of main actors plays the première is decided by chance. The other gets to perform the finale, which is at least as emotional.

Passion season = festival season

The end of the première marks the beginning of a whole series of festivities. Because Passion season is also festival season for the locals. It demands a lot from the people of Oberammergau – time, energy, plenty of nerves. But no one has to worry about their emotional well-being. There is no question of self-flagellation; these people are not mournful by nature, they draw community experience and celebration from this special time. Despite all the international hustle and bustle, they keep their very own traditions away from the tourist spectacle. "There are lots of celebrations around the Passion," says Sophie Schuster. "The première party, the half-time party and the finale party. In between there are always smaller parties that the individual dressing rooms organise. That was very exciting for me in 2010 because for the first time I was allowed to go out and celebrate on my own."

A highlight of all of this is the "Merchants' Party" in summer, which is based on a very special tradition. During the "driving out of the merchants", Jesus angrily casts a giant clay jug weighing thirty kilograms to the floor. In the run-up to the Passion, Barbara Lampe and her sons Tobias and Benjamin produce 130 of them in their pottery, which incidentally was founded in 1903 by her grandfather – Jesus actor Anton Lang. These jugs have a relatively short first life – and a long second life. The first ends when Jesus throws them on the ground. This, it should be noted, is not as impulsive a gesture as it seems: "As Jesus you get instructions from the merchants on how to throw the jug. You can really smash it or just hit it slightly on the edge," says Frederik Mayet. "If you throw it awkwardly, you can pulverise it. But the merchants prefer it when just the handle breaks off." Why? Because of the second life of the jugs. And that second life can only begin once it has been glued back together. To aid this process, they are marked inside with coloured chalk in advance – and Jesus just has to throw them carefully. The broken pieces land on a cloth and are then transported from the stage to the merchants' dressing room. There, the individual parts are put back together over several hours to become a jug once more.

The revived jug is passed through all the dressing rooms to be signed by all performers before being sold. Almost everyone has one of them at home; they can be found in hotels and restaurants. Mayet has the 2010 première jug in his living room. It bears the words "Passion 2010", surrounded by autographs. These souvenirs are priced at a relatively steep 300 euros, but in the end the money benefits everyone. On a non-performance day in summer, the proceeds are used to throw a huge party, the "Merchants' Party". Everything is free – drinks, food, popcorn and ice cream for the children, live music. And suddenly the Passion transforms from an international spectacle to something very local and communal again: a village festival. A little larger than the usual village festival, but a festival nonetheless, held by locals, for locals. With not a tourist to be seen.

The plays put a lot of emphasis on personal responsibility, with the participants quickly developing routines in the Passion season. Because of course, with so many people involved, it is simply impossible to call around. That is why everyone has a duty to be on hand in the theatre for their performance. "It happens backstage," Frederik Mayet tells me. "Everyone knows where their dressing room is and when their turn is. The stage manager doesn't call anyone to the stage by name, he just announces the scenes." And it works. After all, you don't want people staring at you because you screwed up.

There has been double casting for the lead roles in Oberammergau since 1980. The actors decide between themselves who will perform and when in the following week. This schedule goes to the dressing room attendant and someone in charge who always has an overview of the day's cast. In 2010, the two Jesus actors Frederik Mayet and Andreas Richter spoke on the phone every performance day, as Mayet recalls: "'How's your voice? Are you fit? How did you sleep?' Or: 'I'm in Munich today and I have to work, if you can't make it, call me in good time.'" But Mayet never strayed far from the theatre throughout the season from May to October. "There are 5,000 people there, you simply have a responsibility," says Mayet. "To make sure that you are there and ready to go on." Only once did he get cabin fever, and went cycling for a day in Tyrol. He was relieved that he didn't receive an emergency call while he was there.

Christian Stückl, too, can only remember one case in which a leading actor wasn't there. It was in 1990 when the dressing room attendant called him to say that Caiaphas – one of the biggest roles – was missing. Neither of the actors could be reached

The season lasts from May to October. If you're there for almost every performance you need a break from time to time.

by phone, and the first entrance at the end of the first scene was approaching. At some point they reached one of them in Garmisch, who insisted it was not his turn (later the other one said the same thing, by the way, not that it helped). Then Stückl's grandfather Benedikt, who had played the role in 1950 and 1960, stood there and said: "I'll do it". But he was supposed to play the high priest Annas, who appears with Caiaphas. He quickly solved this problem by simply transferring Annas's most important line to the prompter, who is always out on stage in costume. Stückl laughs at the memory: "My grandfather immediately recalled it all, it was very funny. He just set off and went completely back to the 1950 text, which is fifteen minutes longer. He went back thirty years, it was very odd. All the anti-Semitism was back too, everything that I had removed." But it worked. Benedikt Stückl saved the performance. After this experience, Christian Stückl now insists on knowing a week in advance who is on when.

In addition to the adults, five to six hundred children are involved in the Passion. They can be officially registered as soon as they start school. There were three groups of children in 2010, with each regularly assigned to every third play and carrying out stage business such as tending the sheep or performing as servants at the Last Supper. There was a lot of "commotion" in the children's dressing rooms, as Sophie Schuster explains, having experienced it in 2010 at the age of fourteen: "You can just get in there quickly and change, that was relatively fast. Then we would go to the canteen to get a schnitzel roll or a soft drink. And then we always sat in the wings and waited until it started." For the "Entry into Jerusalem" and the "Expulsion of the Merchants", all the children who are assigned that day are there. Between the scenes, "we played practical jokes in the dressing room," Rochus Rückel remembers. Two or three women take care of the children so things don't get completely out of hand. The children do not take part in the difficult scenes, the "Outrage" and the "Crucifixion". Only those who are also appearing in a tableau vivant remain. Or return later. Rückel, for example, was present at the Resurrection in 2010, the last tableau. "That was very practical because you always had an excuse at school if you were tired or you hadn't done your homework," he says with a laugh. "The teachers were really understanding – and of course we shamelessly exploited that."

Standing on the huge stage with friends is a "completely wonderful experience," says Sophie Schuster: "That all those people have come here to see what we're doing." Cengiz Görür also thinks back fondly to 2010 when he and his sister were among the crowd. "Dad called me into his office and said: 'Look, you've received a letter, you can take part in the Passion Play, in the crowd and in a tableau vivant'," he recalls. The kids in his class were all talking about it. Because they were all performing, he did it too. For the Entry into Jerusalem, when Jesus rides in on a donkey, they sang "Heil dir". And in between they would always talk among themselves, very quietly and secretly. Nevertheless, it was stressful having performances again and again from May to October, even during the holidays, when you actually want to go to the swimming pool. But for him, as for the others, the positives predominated. This time all three can be seen in leading roles: as Jesus, Judas and Mary Magdalene. Sophie Schuster is looking forward to it – and she is curious what it will be like to be exposed on stage with just a few others and also to have lines. "In a group you always think you can just blend into the background, that no one really even notices you. Even if that's not true at all. If you stand downstage and look around the audience, they see you."

The animals in the Passion

It's not just adults and children on the Passion Play stage, but animals as well. They may be in the minority, but that doesn't make them any less demanding. Two camels, two horses, a donkey and all kinds of sheep, goats, chickens and pigeons are set to perform in 2022. The larger guest animals are all housed in the meadow behind the Passionstheater with "Scholler Toni", whose real name is Anton Mangold. He takes care of the animals and brings them to the theatre for their performance. At least, he tries. Because they often have their own wills and idiosyncrasies. Take the donkey Sancho, which is strictly speaking a giant Catalan donkey. For the photo shoots in 2020, at one point he had absolutely no desire to go on stage. He simply stopped in front of the theatre, all attempts at motivation failed. It was only when Scholler Toni, who was actually attending a wedding at the time, rushed over that he was persuaded to make his entrance.

To get the camels onto the stage, you need a "camel driving licence". Scholler Toni spent a fortnight on the camel farm in Landsberg where the animals come from, to get to know them and gain the necessary certification. They are actually very humble animals, he explains. They have no problem with the cold in the mountains; it can often get much colder in the desert. The only thing they are not prepared for is snow, "because they have no claws, just a hoof, so they slide around teddy bears," says Scholler. And if there is a thunderstorm, forget about it. "If a camel decides to be stubborn, you won't shift it. If they don't want to move, that's it," he says. Perhaps that is why not all participants share his view of the animals' character. "Camels are the craftiest animals I know," says Markus Köpf, who appeared as Herod with them in 2010. "They always come across as crumpled, but they are very shady beasts." They also spit, bite or kick whenever they feel like it. Or they stand facing the wall with Herod's servant on their back, rather than the audience. "But by and large, they also love the limelight," says Köpf. "So it usually goes quite well."

The greatest challenge, however, is the horses. There are meant to be two this time, so that the captain and Pilate can ride on stage together and demonstrate Roman power. Which they do. "It does something to you when you ride in," says Köpf, who plays the captain this time. "You are immediately the king of the castle, everyone has to look up to you. The elevated seating position is a power factor over the crowd. Everyone makes sure that they don't get too close to you. The biggest nobody can be someone on a horse." He laughs. In the meantime he has got used to riding. In 2010 it was different. When Christian Stückl announced to him

Not only do all the human performers need to be on stage on time, but the animals too. They have their own entrance with a ramp.

that he would ride as Herod this time (and not just as the captain as he had previously), he didn't take it seriously. Or, he suppressed it. Because he had nothing to do with horses, didn't even want to ride a pony when he went to the zoo as a child. Until he was out walking one day and bumped into his Herod colleague, who was riding a horse with a riding instructor by his side. He realised that the riding was no joke. "I was already eight weeks behind," he recalls. So he took lessons as well; after all, he didn't want to show himself up.

At the first photo rehearsal in 2010 he was still "sweating like never before" in his life. The Passion horse Gerko, which was 1.80 metres tall and significantly larger than his training horses, had never seen a camel before. When the two humped animals appeared next to him on the stage, he was uncomfortable. The horse was nervous, which didn't necessarily make life easier for its rider, who was also nervous. This time, Köpf is better prepared for his appearance on horseback, knows what to look out for and passes this knowledge on to his riding colleagues. One of them is Anton Preisinger, who will play Pilate and who also has concerns about it. The fact that his father waved to him from his horse as a Roman captain in 1970 helps his morale, but nothing more. "Riding isn't really my hobby," admits Preisinger. "But now the role demands it." In December 2019 he started riding lessons, which this time took place in a group. Now he will probably get back in the saddle in winter. His riding scene is fairly short, which is a comfort; he rides on the stage with the captain, the soldiers drive the crowd out, and then he can dismount again. "I just hope that there aren't too many riding experts in the audience, because of course they'll see straight away that I'm a complete beginner," he says with a laugh.

In the run-up to the current Passion, the donkey, which has always been part of the Entry into Jerusalem, caused a stir. The animal welfare organisation PETA approached the then Oberammergau mayor Arno Nunn and Walter Rutz, manager of the in-house company Oberammergau Kultur, and requested that they dispense with the donkey (and all other animals) entirely. "Nowadays Jesus would no longer ride a donkey," says Peter Höffken, specialist at PETA. "He would probably get around on an e-scooter or another animal-friendly and environmentally friendly electric vehicle."[90] This suggestion was not implemented, but they made a conscious decision in favour of the giant Catalan donkey because it is particularly powerful. And it's not like Jesus covers a lot of distance on him either. Frederik Mayet, one of the Jesus actors, estimates it's about thirty metres from the back to the stage. And if you read the descriptions of Anton Lang, who rode the donkey as Jesus in 1900, 1910 and 1922, there certainly seem to be animals who enjoy acting – and who want to remind their human colleagues who is really is the stronger among them. "[The donkey] was soon so familiar with the play that when his time came, he trotted to the theatre by himself and presented himself in his own language at the back entrance," Lang writes in his memoir. "He couldn't stand teasing. One fellow performer had teased him with a sugar lump before the performance, and out on stage during a tableau vivant, he stepped so hard on the actor's bare foot, for which of course the sandal offered no protection, that he had to grit his teeth to stay in place."[91]

Turbulence

Even with the best planning in the world, when you have so many people and animals involved more or less in the open air, you're going to have the odd mistake. The auditorium is covered, but not the stage. It only has an emergency roof that can be extended if necessary. On one day in 2010, Christian Stückl was not in Oberammergau, but rather at a rehearsal for "Jedermann" at the Salzburg Festival, Mayet recalls. It was a wonderful summer day, but – with the kind of sudden climatic change typical of mountain regions – a thunderstorm whipped up. The retractable roof was not extended in time. "It was in the middle of the Mount of Olives scene in the afternoon, and suddenly it started to hail," says Mayet. "I didn't know how to deal with it. Someone in the first row was hit and had a laceration. Then I went to the others and said we should stop the performance. That was a difficult situation, we had never discussed stopping, there was such an internal hurdle to overcome. I mean, there are plays where it's easier to do. That really upset me." Fortunately, after a short break, the play was able to continue. Also in 1990, one afternoon there was such a violent thunderstorm that the rain and thunder smothered every line. "It poured, it all came down, there was thunder and lightning," says Christian Stückl. "It all started with the Crucifixion.

Paramedics removed seventeen people from the auditorium who had fainted because it was so real. I was standing in the auditorium and I was overwhelmed that Heaven was suddenly playing along without us even requesting it."

In 2000 they accidentally skipped an entire scene, which put the following scenes under stress, because there were now ten minutes missing from the play and performers usually only get to the theatre just in time for their scene. So then they had to ring round and tell everyone to come earlier. The scene changes are always risky moments. When a change is pending – and this is quite often the case with the twelve tableaux vivants – the entire rear performance area is pushed away on wheels to make space for the frames in which the tableaux vivants are arranged. The stage workers have just two and a half minutes to do all this before the participants have to move into position and the curtain opens again. It's quite an athletic exercise, and backstage things are at least as turbulent as they are out front. There have certainly been occasions when the choir is singing about a tableau vivant but the curtain can't open, because chaos still reigns behind, Carsten Lück admits with a smile. "But that's the exception."

The last performance is another very special occasion, even if it seems at first like all the others. Before it begins, the Catholic and Protestant pastors take turns leading the participants in the Lord's Prayer. Then the performance begins. But unlike normal performances, when the ensemble departs the stage without bowing at the end, which is not appropriate for a religious play, at the end of the last performance everyone comes on stage, even those who haven't performed that day. All the doors are opened for the Hallelujah, and there are around 2000 people on the stage. They rehearse the entrances and exits specially beforehand, otherwise it would be totally impossible. Everyone sings "Shema Yisrael"

The first rehearsal of the Crucifixion in 2020 turns out to be the last crowd rehearsal for the year. Days later, the play is postponed.

and "Great God We Praise You" again, Christian Stückl gives a speech. "There are so many tears, on stage and in the auditorium. Everyone claps along, it's simply the end of a great strain, a relief as well," says Monika Lang, describing the mixed feelings of the evening. At the closing party that follows, some performers get rid of their beard and hair there and then – and everyone farewells the Passion season. "Then there's a void," says Frederik Mayet. "It's crazy, from one day to the next the village is totally empty. The tourists are gone, everyone is exhausted and many people go on holidays. But you know: it will start again in ten years."

THE NEW PLAGUE.
CORONA AND THE POSTPONEMENT
OF THE PLAY

In Oberammergau, until 2020 the fact that "the Passion" takes place every ten years was as certain as the amen in church. Corona has shaken some of those certainties. The pulse of the place, as the Passion rhythm was once called, stopped. There have been no irregularities in the Passion programme since the Second World War: they take place every ten years, and there were even additional plays in 1977 and 1984. For almost everyone involved this time, even the village elders, the experience of the postponement is something new. Something that you only know about from history and theory.

On 8 March 2020 I am heading to Oberammergau again. About a week earlier, while attending a première at the Münchner Kammerspiele, for the first time I sense a tension in everything, and that some people are taking care not to get too close to others. A few days later there is a press conference for the "Radikal jung" festival in the Münchner Volkstheater. In the midst of the discussion, the unbelievable question arises for the first time: "When will the theatres be closed?" The seemingly antiquated word "quarantine" is used for the first time in schools. Children who were in South Tyrol (Italy) during the Carnival holiday are not allowed to come for two weeks. So it is a strangely insecure mood when I drive to Oberammergau. Two months after the first big stage rehearsal.

Again it is cold, again they're rehearsing in anoraks. Rochus Rückel pulls the huge wooden Cross onto the stage. He drags it rather than carries it, collapsing several times under the load. This is the day of the first Crucifixion rehearsal. Rückel is placed

In March 2020 Christian Stückl announced that the play would be postponed by two years.

on the Cross, fastened and pulled up. For the first time he hangs high above those who want to see the "King of the Jews" dead and those who weep for him. And for the last time this year. Because this first Crucifixion rehearsal is also the last major rehearsal for the Oberammergau Passion Play 2020. Because of the corona pandemic, the rehearsals have to be cancelled shortly afterwards and the play postponed by two years.

Standstill

On 19 March 2020, what quite a few had suspected or feared for a long time became certain: director Christian Stückl was forced to announce that the 2020 Passion Play was to be postponed to 2022 due to the corona pandemic. Three days earlier, Bavarian Minister-President Markus Söder had declared a state of emergency in Bavaria, everything that is not absolutely essential is closed. "I just didn't have a good feeling about it any more," said Christian Stückl to the few press representatives who had come to Oberammergau in front of the Passionstheater. The local council had unanimously decided the evening before not to cancel the play, but to postpone it. "We will continue at some point and we are in good spirits," said Stückl. His voice halted and tears came to his eyes. Seeing that was hard for many, including Monika Lang. "The consequences this has for the individual, for the village and the world … For everyone who wanted to come and everyone who would have participated. It was like a soap bubble bursting."

Up until two days before the decision Stückl was talking about "perseverance", as he told me a little later on the phone, even though he had already suspected that the risk had become too great. "Even my main actors didn't really believe it any more, I saw some tears. When the cancellation came, it really hit me emotionally." Before he announced the decision from the Garmisch-Partenkirchen district administration to the press, he called his core ensemble together. Only a few came. The disappointment was too great.

Instead of starting the final rehearsals, Oberammergau – like Bavaria, Germany and almost the whole world – came to a standstill. Costumes, props and backdrops were labelled, packed and mothballed. Instead of continuing with rehearsals, Christian

Stückl gave interviews and "wound down" his play. Half a million tickets had to be cancelled or rebooked. He sounded quieter than usual on the phone, thwarted. In early March 2020, he realised that not everything would happen as planned. "I had a big rehearsal with 400 people," he recalled. "And then it really hit me that I had too many old people on stage, that it was dangerous." The next day he called the mayor and said that he needed a council meeting to discuss how things were to proceed. "We have up to 1,000 people on stage and over 4,000 in the auditorium. We just needed an assessment from the district administrator and the health department," says Stückl. He cancelled the planned rehearsals for the time being.

"You can't do theatre like that, under these circumstances. You can't be linguistically precise and refine scenes," explained Stückl. "Ultimately, we all agreed that the postponement was sad, but also a liberation after the to and fro." They briefly discussed rescheduling the play for 2021, but 2022 seemed more realistic. At the time, no one knew when the situation around the world would return to normal. Now, over a year later, it turns out that it was the only course of action; the play would certainly not have been possible in 2021. Even now, in autumn 2021, it is not entirely clear what the situation will be at the start of rehearsals in winter, whether and what restrictions there will be over the next year.

Pandemic revival

It is not the first time that the Passion Play has been postponed. And not the first time that this has happened because of a pandemic. The Passion of 1920 could not take place until 1922. Because many had not returned from World War I or were still in captivity. And because the Spanish flu broke out in what was already a highly difficult situation. At that time, too, cancellation was out of the question: "In 1921 [...] people in Oberammergau seriously considered whether it would be better to wait until 1930. With a twenty-year break, the young people would not have had any contact with the play."[92] What was valid then was also valid in 2020. "There have always been difficult phases in history. But from this you can also see that life goes on and things are looking up again," said Frederik Mayet in the summer of 2021. "Right now things are difficult because of corona, but it is all the more important to do the 2022 play. If we only picked it up again in 2030 and had no play for twenty years, there would be a real void for both participants and visitors. A complete cancellation would be a real break." A cancellation would also mean a generation of children who lack this formative experience. A generation that would not be considered as the next generation later on because they have nothing in common with this theatre.

What's more, the Passion Play has become a guarantor of stability in the village over the centuries. Things will never be so bad that there is no Passion. There is barely anything that could keep the people of Oberammergau from holding on to their play. Not bans (even if these came from the church and actually released them from their vows). Not wars (only the Second World War was of a dimension they couldn't contend with). Not even epidemics. Nevertheless, the unpredictability of the corona pandemic has shaken the village deeply. That a new disease, of all things, could bring the play to a standstill in the 21st century, when it was supposed to protect against things like that. For quite a few villagers, the first impulse was: we have to do it, especially in this situation, that is precisely our vow, that is our mission. Andreas Richter described this impulse in a podcast at Easter 2021:

"There was a lot of talk about the fact that we can't just let it go. […] This belief, this deep inner connection with something bigger than ourselves, can be healing. This can be an important resource in a time when you have to defend yourself against a virus."[93]

The belief in the play, which in Oberammergau is always two things – the (religious) tradition and the communal making of theatre – puts the individual in a larger context, makes them part of the bigger picture, provides support in difficult times. The 2022 play is something like a light at the end of the tunnel. This is important. Because staging the play demands more of people today than in earlier times. Many study or no longer work in the village and have to plan their entire life around the Passion every ten years. Corona has thrown a few lives and life planning into disarray. It is one thing to be prepared for one exceptional year every decade with a long lead time. It is a different matter altogether to then reschedule this exceptional year for two years later. To up-end lives into Passion mode twice within three years. And in a situation that is difficult for everyone professionally, even without the Passion. In which many have lost their jobs or been furloughed, in which many certainties have been lost. In our conversation after the cancellation, Christian Stückl told me that he would like to keep the cast if at all possible. "I very much hope that everyone will be there again. Let's see how it turns out."

Re-rescheduling

Even if it is difficult, everyone I spoke to naturally wants to be there in 2022 as well. Even if it means rescheduling studies, re-organising your work again, applying for a sabbatical or unpaid leave once more. Christoph Stöger, who will play John, had postponed his first state law examination for the Passion 2020. Now he will start his legal internship later so he can take part in 2022. "When I tell friends who are not from Oberammergau, they say it's completely insane," he says. "Many of them can't really understand how you can revolve your life and your planning around it like that. But you grow up with it, you take part as a child and realise what a great thing it is."

Eva Reiser got to play Mary Magdalene in 2010 and is now Mary. To be cast twice in a leading role is an even greater honour for a woman than for a man, with female roles notoriously few and far between; after a certain age there are none at all. The postponement has thrown Reiser's planning up in the air. Everything was organised for 2020 and had to be changed again. So she needs a new plan for 2022. Now, in the summer of 2021, she still doesn't know exactly what form it will take. "After the experience of the postponement, I'm more cautious this time and I am trying to postpone the decision as long as possible," she says. Of course, in the back of your mind there is the question of whether you can ask your employer for a special exemption again. Of course, people are more cautious. Nevertheless, the option of giving up the role is no option at all. "I want to do it now," she says. "Sure, it would be easier to organise it all if I were one of the crowd, but if you have been selected it is not enough, you want to perform the role."

At the beginning, Sophie Schuster "pushed the corona issue away for as long as possible and thought that things would work out." When they didn't, "everything was suddenly thrown overboard. It was pretty hard at the beginning," she recalls in the summer of 2021. "It took me a while to realise – that was it for the year." She continued her remote marketing studies, but financially she had planned around the Passion, of course. So she reapplied to the bank where she did her training. She got a job and became "a little more relaxed" again. She did not find it easy during the long stand-by mode imposed by the postponement. "You always have in the back of your head, 2022 is Passion, you plan everything with this in mind." So she is looking forward with even greater anticipation to the moment when the rehearsals finally kick off again.

For a long time Rochus Rückel did not want to admit that anything might happen to the Passion 2020. "There came a point where you noticed – this is an emergency," he tells me in retrospect. "Overall, the mood was still quite positive, we thought it would work out." It was his birthday on 14 March, the day when photos were taken for the illustrated book. He was in the canteen when all participants were summoned onto the stage by an announcement. "You never have announcements like that," he says. "So we all knew what it meant." That is, the end of the rehearsals. Rückel did not even come to the official cancellation. He took the risk of infection very seriously and was "very worried that people around me would get infected and get sick". Which luckily didn't happen. "But the cancellation of the Passion was actually quite bearable," he says in his thoughtful manner. "It was a matter of life and death."

Still, it was strange when his whole daily schedule collapsed from one day to the next. One day everything is fully booked up with rehearsals and studying for exams at uni. Then suddenly everything was gone. Rückel helped his brother restore a Unimog truck in their home workshop and wrote his bachelor thesis. He was supposed to have been doing that in parallel with the play, which would have been "very intense". He hadn't allowed himself a semester off from his aerospace studies for the Passion, which in retrospect was a good idea. So he was able to write without interruption under lockdown – and will probably be working on his master's thesis during the Passion in 2022. It seems there's no getting away from that dual workload.

All loyalty to the Passion notwithstanding, some changes in the line-up are unavoidable. There will be 138 participants who can no longer take part in 2022. Some have died, others have made other plans. But others have joined, some of whom did not have time in 2020, others who only became eligible to perform after the postponement. One of them is Ulrike Bubenzer. On her mother's side, her family has deep roots in Oberammergau, tracing their origins back to the vow. But since she grew up in Munich and only moved back to Oberammergau in 2001, she will not have the right to perform until 2022. Incidentally, nobody lost their performing right as a result of the postponement; everyone who was under 18 years of age in 2020 and had the right to perform a children's part can also take part in 2022. Once cast, you cannot be kicked out.

In Oberammergau, the theatre is an economic factor. The outdoor swimming pool, among other things, was built with the surplus from the Passion. "*Passion wirds scho richten*," they say here when things get tight – "Passion will fix it". The hotels are fully booked in the round years, the restaurants generate more sales than in the preceding nine years, and guests buy souvenirs and merchandise. Every ten years the Passion fills up the coffers (and that is why every dispute about the Passion is always at least partly a dispute about money). In Oberammergau people live off tourism, and the Passion season is without question high season. "We depend on it," as then head of the main municipal administration, Martin Norz, said to Ilja Trojanow in 2010. "Maintaining the facilities we have here has become a big problem because we have little else. There isn't enough tourism in the intervening years; the sports facilities, ski lifts, the wave pool […], all of this is financed by the Passion Play years."[94] Here, too, the deferral has brought big changes. On the large scale (in the municipality) as well as on the small scale (retail, hotels and restaurants).

Oberammergau's prosperity is based to a large extent on the play and everything related to it. Cengiz Görür, whose father runs a hotel in Oberammergau, confirms to me how difficult it was after the postponement; instead of a full house there was suddenly a ghost town. Overnight, a season that was completely booked out was replaced by an empty calendar. Lockdown instead of a rush of tourists. The fact that things weren't quite as bad as originally feared is due to the fact that accommodation for travel within Germany was permitted again in early summer 2020. So Oberammergau benefited from the many residents who spontaneously took holidays in their own country because they couldn't travel abroad.

Planning in uncertainty

The 2022 play is being planned in the shadow of uncertainty. When the play was postponed, the world was locked down. When advance sales for 2022 began in October 2020, there was still no vaccine. But there were plenty of hygiene regulations for theatres and distancing rules on the stage – ten square metres per person. Extrapolated to conditions in Oberammergau, where around 1,000 people perform at the same time, this would have entailed a stage one hectare in size … and you can forget about the orchestra. At the press conference for the launch of advance sales, neither Christian Stückl nor managing director Walter Rutz denied the uncertainties. Will corona be over in 2022? Will people be travelling again? Will foreign guests be able to enter the country? Nobody knew any of this at the time. Still, they wanted to take an optimistic approach. As did the audience – around fifty percent of the tickets booked for 2022 up to summer 2021 are re-bookings from 2020.

Nevertheless, it is a production taking place under great uncertainty. What will be allowed when the rehearsals start again in December? Exactly when in May 2022 is the première? Suddenly, the functioning of the play is no longer in the hands of the Oberammergau residents; it depends on external circumstances. If they have to impose hygiene measures, not everyone will be able to perform, says Stückl. "Then we would have to tell five or six hundred people that they have to stay at home." And who should that be? The older ones who would love to play again but have already taken part six, seven or eight times? Or the young ones who are meant to carry the Passion into the future? "It's going to be a huge battle," says Stückl. "How do you decide who can take part and who can't? Someone is definitely going to be disappointed." At least the situation in the auditorium seems to have been clarified to some extent, with the plays expected to take place under 2G or 3G specifications (2G means audience members must be either vaccinated or recovered; 3G additionally allows for presentation of negative test results no more than 24 hours old).

And what about the play itself? What will that be like in 2022? What changes will the experience of the pandemic bring? How will it differ from 2020? In summer 2021, Christian Stückl is clear: "We don't know how 2020 would have turned out. But 2022 will definitely be different." He will sit down again with the text, listen to it and to himself. See what still fits. And what doesn't. A lot has changed since his first Passion. "I notice that the text bores me in the parts where it becomes highly theological; where, for example, they discuss the observance of the Sabbath," Stückl tells me. "So I have to take another look now, because interpersonal relationships are increasingly important to me. For me, the religious ballast recedes into the background, the social comes to the fore." He is increasingly interested in what happens between individuals rather than conflicts between religions.

During the pandemic, he was shocked by how many theatre practitioners kept emphasising the "systemic relevance" of art and how they hated being thrown together with brothels and restaurants. "At some point it really ticked me off," says Stückl. "For some reason nobody was interested in how those people were doing and that the gap between rich and poor was growing all the time. Everyone was just looking out for themselves. And in the end we probably don't even care about the climate, the main thing is that we can go on holiday again." Naturally there is an urgency to the story of someone who sticks to fundamental values. Stückl has long been aware that Jesus is someone who can annoy, who can push people until they're white-hot with anger. He is an "imposition", as he once put it. Because he never stops reminding people who they could be. If only they wanted it. What they could and should change.

TIME FOR UTOPIAS.
THE FUTURE OF THE PASSION PLAY

The new pandemic came at a time when everything seemed to have settled down to some extent. The preparations for the 2020 play took place in unusual harmony, there were no referendums and no major protests. It was rare to have so little friction. Most of the people in the village have now realised that the changes that Stückl made were important in bringing the play into the new millennium. They have such trust in him for his fourth Passion that they no longer discuss every staging idea in the local council. Success has proven him right.

The Passion Play has received more national and international recognition in the past ten years than ever before. In 2020/21 alone, Stückl was awarded three prizes for his commitment to tolerance and the fight against anti-Semitism. He was awarded the Abraham Geiger Prize, the Tolerance Prize of the Evangelical Academy in Tutzing and, most recently, the Buber Rosenzweig Medal. In 2014 the Passion Play became an example of "Intangible Cultural Heritage", and in 2020 the *New York Times* added the Oberammergau play to its list of "52 Places to Go in 2020". In November 2020 the community finally made the former "Stage Terror" an honorary citizen. "The municipal council would like to thank Mr Christian Stückl as a citizen and personality of Oberammergau and as a person with deep roots in the village for his extremely positive and successful work internally and externally and for acting as an ambassador for the Passion Play and to express our appreciation by granting honorary citizenship", said the official statement of the municipal council. A sign of reconciliation after all the fighting.

How much tradition is too much?

Stückl has taken the play to a new level. The younger generation of performers only knows the Passion under his direction. For them, the disputes over his selection, the trench warfare between traditionalists and innovators are history. Anti-Semitism seems to have been overcome as far as possible. If you ask the young people in Oberammergau about their motivation, they are very enthusiastic. "I took part when I was three, I can't really remember that, and then when I was 13. And that was it for me," says Kilian Clauß, for example. "Since then, it has been very easy for me to rave about the Passion because it was such a great time." In 2017 he himself led rehearsals for the annual Nativity play with the children, which is of course a bigger thing in Oberammergau than anywhere else. "I asked Christian [Stückl] if I could do it. Since he's always notoriously too busy himself, he agreed." Clauß also took on this task in the following years, now he's assistant director of the Passion and playing Nathanael.

Sophie Schuster took on the female title role in the interim production of "Romeo and Juliet" under Abdullah Kenan Karaca in 2015 – and now she is Mary Magdalene in the Passion. She does not believe "that it will come to the point that this tradition will end". And Rochus Rückel is also looking positively to the future. "We now have the youngest line-up ever, so it is in very good hands for the future." No trace of a crisis of legitimacy, in other words. Which is without doubt due to the fact that Stückl and his colleagues do not keep young people down, rather they let them grow up alongside them, take care of them and, by promoting young talent, show they really understand what promotion means. Not just discovering talent, but actively facilitating careers. It seems to have become part of the tradition that pro-

There is no lack of young talent and motivation in Oberammergau. There will be people who grow into the calling of the Passion.

fessionals keep their eyes peeled for talent. Even today, a comparatively large number of people from Oberammergau end up in professional theatre.

Lorenz Stöger, who performed in the Passion as a child in 2000 and 2010, studies stage design at the Weißensee Kunsthochschule Berlin and is assisting Stefan Hageneier in the current play. Cengiz Görür applied to study acting at the Otto Falckenberg School in Munich in 2020. He was one of very few accepted. Abdullah Kenan Karaca performed in the Passion 2000 as a child. After graduating from high school, he studied directing at the University of Music and Theatre in Hamburg. Today he works as a director and in 2020/22 as the deputy director in Oberammergau. Would any of them have gone into theatre without the Passion

Play? It's questionable, to say the least. And the fact that a student like Stöger is so matter-of-fact about his expectation of performing in the Passion when he's ninety shows how deeply the place is rooted in its theatre tradition.

But one thing is becoming increasingly difficult for the next generation: reconciling Passion with life planning. When Christian Stückl ordered another cappuccino in the theatre café in 2021, he asked the young waiter, what did he think about the 2030 or 2040 Passion? Stückl considers his answer to be more or less typical: he certainly wants to, but he is currently studying medicine in Salzburg. Where will he be in eight years? No idea. Christoph Stöger, Lorenz's brother, gave me a similar answer. "Of course I want to perform, but I have to see where I am and what I am doing for work then, how it can be arranged," he says. "It's relatively easy still, I'm a student, young and independent. But the next Passion will probably present us all with the biggest struggle to take part." Do you stay in Oberammergau? Do you start a family elsewhere? What if your partner is not from Oberammergau and is not allowed to perform? Next time, today's highly active generation will be at what is probably the most difficult point in the Passion biography: in the middle of family and career planning.

Eva Reiser also believes that some things will change, that it cannot "work forever the way we do it now. They need to look at maybe working with professionals and students. They may need to relax things or approach them differently to keep it feasible. The motivation and fascination will remain. The only question is: how do you manage to always bring it into the near future, so that everyone can participate?" Stückl also recognises this problem: "Structurally, we actually only have tourism and two or three clinics around the village. Everything else is far away, more and more people work in Munich." The young people are moving away for their careers. Exactly the ones that Passion so desperately needs.

Who is an Oberammergauer?

So if the good players move away and the others who move here are not allowed to participate due to the performance right, it will be difficult to maintain the quality. "We will need to let go of some things," thinks Stückl. "And it's good to let them go." For example: the twenty-year rule. A restriction that arose from the spirit of excluding all newcomers. An exclusionary gesture that is no longer in keeping with the times, believes Stückl. He sees the systematic exclusion of all "newcomers", whether from Weilheim or Syria, as a relic from a bygone era that has to be overcome. In the interludes he notices what or who is missing from the Passion. Here, anyone who lives in Oberammergau can perform. No matter how long they've lived there. "Then suddenly you have people who have just arrived here, like Raouf Habibi, who lives with my family. There is also a woman who moved here nineteen years ago and sang in the choir at every interlude – but she's one year short for the Passion, so she's out," explains Stückl. The question, "Who is an Oberammergauer?", will have to be answered in the future by: "Anyone who lives here."

If the twenty-year rule is actually lifted one day, the right to perform may also have to go. Essentially there are already too many taking part, says Stückl: "Sometimes the scenes are so jammed with the masses. We may have to have double casting for everyone, even the crowds and the soldiers. Then you can have more people, and the stage is still a bit clearer." And if there is no other way, you just have to draw lots. Then at least nobody is

Perhaps the next director is already in the starting blocks?

excluded from the start. "We are in a state of upheaval," believes Stückl. "But where exactly we will land we don't yet know."

Passion post Stückl?

And then there is the one question that nobody here really wants to ask: who could take over the direction of the play in ten or twenty years? Stückl has set a high bar. He will be a hard act to follow. "I don't know the Passion without Christian and I don't really want to imagine," says Eva Reiser, echoing the sentiments of many. "Of course he will say it has to go on, a younger person has to do it. And he's right. It's not up to him, I'm sure he'd be willing to give up his post to someone who wants to do that. But somehow there's no screaming as long as he's here." The former revolutionary has become a classic; the new beginning in terms of personnel is the next challenge. "It will just be completely different," says Reiser. "You have to let go of the thought that it will continue in the same way."

The job for the new generation will not be to tackle outdated ideas, but rather to break away from the great role model Stückl one day and find their own way. What Holzheimer wrote about the Passion 2000 applies to them as well: "Tradition is not static because stasis cannot be tradition in itself. Tradition, in its literal sense, is something that is handed down, passed on and therefore subject to change. [...] Again and again [...] people pretend that there is a tradition per se and not just its dynamic appropriation."[95]

Only then will the play remain a vivid confrontation with history and the text, rather than a museum of local history. Stückl himself is not the kind of person to believe that once you do something it is perpetually valid. If this spirit can be preserved, if they don't just put one production into mothballs and dust it off every ten years, then this Passion will remain relevant. Theatre is a fleeting art which arises on the stage in one moment and fades away in the next, only to reinvent itself – in this case ten years later. Or as Otto Huber put it in 1990: "As in other areas of life [...] with the Passion Play, too, the fact that you have already done something can give you confidence that you will repeat it again, but it is not necessarily easier by definition. The Passion Play is not an icon or a museum piece that can be passed on as such without reference to the present; it has to be created over and over again. The melody that is played here can only be sounded on the strings of one's own life – the Passion only lives if the participants bring it to life through themselves."[96]

At some point they will need to find someone with the desire to take on this mammoth task, which takes a lot of strength and nerves, but can also be addictive. Someone from Oberammergau. Someone who knows their stuff and loves it despite all the quirks. Someone who has good ideas and can handle conflict. Because making the Passion not only requires good ideas and commitment, but also a good deal of resilience and assertiveness. Maybe there will be a dry spell before a new approach emerges. Christian Stückl looks to the future with his signature curiosity, but he doesn't have a specific suggestion at the moment. "I don't know who's going to do it," he says in the summer of 2021. "You can't cultivate it. I always ask myself, where is the boy or girl who wants to do this one day? I think it would be really exciting if a young woman came and said she'd like to be a Passion Play director."

A woman as Passion Play director? That would be a logical progression. In theory, of course, initially. Because the young women I spoke to have no such ambitions. And beyond the management positions (staging, music, sets and costumes), the potential for making the Passion more feminine are highly constrained. Of course you can't make a woman out of Jesus, and the apostles weren't women either. And the women of Oberammergau do not want to take on male roles either; in this respect they remain true to history. The narrative, which is clearly male-dominated, limits the options here. "You can't just keep inventing tons of female roles," agrees Reiser. "But it would be nice if the existing women got a little more text." Andrea Hecht, who played Mary in 2010, complains that the women's texts were "very superficial". "I would like them to have a little more content. You don't have to give a sermon."[97] Monika Lang shares this opinion. "The few women who are in it could take on a different significance. The women just don't have much to say, not enough comes across." Mary Magdalene in particular has more potential as an important woman among the apostles. Perhaps you just have to get a little creative. "Of course there is very little in the Bible about women, it hardly noticed that they were there at all," says Andrea Hecht. "But I think that was also a fact of the time. If you weren't allowed to talk about women back then, if you didn't want them to say anything publicly, then you absolutely have to now."[98]

In Oberammergau, after centuries of struggle, people have come to see the Passion Play as a play, as a drama. The idea that only Christians can be part of this religious play has been overcome. "You don't have to be a believer to portray a character from the Bible," says Eva Reiser. "I think the question of religiosity is a little outdated." Christian values are also evident in togetherness: peaceful coexistence with others, tolerance, respect and mutual appreciation. The ideal of the play has long been enlightening: all people are equal and have the same rights. Performing together also creates social utopias on a small scale. In this place (theatrical) art has always been a catalyst for all the conflicts that arise between people (or groups). Global conflicts emerge in a concentrated form, as if under a magnifying glass. As such this Passion Play, which resembles a popular assembly, is more than just theatre – it is also the image of a changing society, democracy in microcosm.

So in Oberammergau they're slowly getting closer to the ideal that one's own biography and origin do not play a role in casting, only acting talent and personality; while here the view is widening, elsewhere it is just getting narrower. In 2021 Amazon Studios started their own debate about who can play whom. However, the impulse to protect minorities has given rise to a requirement that basically means the end of theatre, the performing arts. The new guidelines stipulate that actors should match their roles in terms of gender, gender identity, nationality, ethnicity, sexual orientation and disability. You could put it another way: everyone is only allowed to play themselves. The requirement is not that nobody should be excluded on the basis of a personal – and private – characteristic, but rather that he or she *has* to have this or that characteristic to get a role. Such a regulation would be the end of the Passion Play; hardly anyone here comes from the Middle East, and no Oberammergau woman has ever experienced a virgin birth. The characters in the play have precious little in common with their performers.

The basic question is: what is more important? Dealing with relevant topics or a cast that is supposedly correct, but denies any ability of an actor or actress to appropriate another person's life? The theatre of the future will have to confront these questions. And so will the Passion Play. After everything I've learned about Oberammergau over the past two years, I have no doubt what the answer will be here. The people of Oberammergau will continue to grapple with stories that have little to do with their own lives, that are located in a different part of the world, at a completely different time. By studying them, future generations will also ask questions. Questions that will enrich coexistence in this not exactly tiny village in the foothills of the Alps. Enrich it with dialogue, food for thought, broadened perspectives, empathy with the fates of others. Nobody here can imagine an end to this tradition. Things are looking good for the next four hundred years.

EPILOGUE

While I was writing this book, the world changed. It took a break and quietly turned back a few rounds. Centuries-old anti-Semitic conspiracies were revived by self-proclaimed *Querdenker*, or "lateral thinkers", and old hatreds re-fuelled. At first, it seemed like the world was moving closer together in the face of its mutual threat, because suddenly everyone had the same problems (and no solution). Poor countries and rich, north, south, east and west. The whole world was in lockdown. But very soon the differences became apparent. How well or how badly a country coped with the pandemic said a lot about its structures and opportunities, and about the distribution of resources. How scientific knowledge was accepted or denied said a lot about the nature of humans.

The corona pandemic has lasted longer than most of us could have imagined in spring 2020. Because we lacked the experience of what an aggressive virus can do in a globally networked world. When I wrote the prologue, schools and theatres had just closed for a few weeks, and it felt like a long time. Naively, I (and quite a few others I spoke to) expected that after these weeks we would be able to return to normal. Fortunately, the Oberammergauers were smart enough to put in a buffer and postpone their play by two years (smarter than the Olympic Committee, for instance.)

This book was written during a strange time when it became the exception for children to go to school and adults to go to the office. Instead, everything took place at home at the same time: home-schooling, working from home, cabin fever. On the one hand you had a very close-knit huddle, on the other, you were socially distanced from anyone who did not belong to this intimate circle, which was suddenly called "one household".

Unfamiliar proximity and unfamiliar separation, all at the same time.

Since March 2020, doing things as a group has carried a sense of something dangerous; a crowd of people seems like a threat. This experience also shaped the creation of the current Passion Play. Not only did the play arise out of a crisis, it also deals with the ultimate crisis in the life of Jesus, a crisis of faith. For Christian Stückl, its message is clear: "Show your colours. Like an Easter egg. Reject those who put others down. And get up again after difficult situations."[99] Overcoming the fear of the pandemic, returning to the value of community – that too makes the Passion Play 2022 a symbol of hope and belief in the future. A future after the pandemic. Perhaps this is why this 42nd play is closer to its origins than it has been in most years.

(October 2021)

ACKNOWLEDGEMENTS

A big thank you to Frederik Mayet, who not only believed in this book straight away, but also told me so much about Oberammergau and the Passion Play in many conversations both short and long. Christian Stückl also always took the time to talk, even if he never actually had the time. Between the Münchner Volkstheater moving to its new home, rehearsals and a well-deserved summer break, he talked to me for one Saturday afternoon in the theatre café about his path to the Passion, the past and the future. *Merci beaucoup.*

Without this openness, which so many other Oberammergau residents extended to me, I would never have been able to write this book. Many thanks to David Bender, Ulrike Bubenzer, Kilian Clauß, Stefan Hageneier, Cengiz Görür, Markus Köpf, Monika Lang, Carsten Lück, Florian Maderspacher, Anton Preisinger, Anton Preisinger Jr., Eva Reiser, Andreas Richter, Andreas Rödl, Rochus Rückel, Scholler Toni, Sophie Schuster, Alexander Schwarz, Christoph Stöger, Lorenz Stöger, Peter Stückl and Markus Zwink for all the anecdotes and a glimpse behind the scenes. And to Ludwig Mödl, who helped me clarify some theological questions.

Jenny Greza and Franziska Seher answered all of my questions, measured the Cross for me and established contacts. Thank you to the in-house company Oberammergau Kultur and manager Walter Rutz for supplying many of the photos here. Cornelia Pichler put together statistics on births and deaths for me. Michaela Prisco and Julia Borghoff read an early version of my manuscript, encouraged me and removed my doubts. Jessica Krämer, Detlev Baur, Oliver Brunner and my parents read and gave me helpful tips. Johanna Deffner sent me the text from 1960 simply because she knew that I was interested in Oberammergau. Paul Tischler and Nicole Gronemeyer from Verlag Theater der Zeit were interested in this book before it existed and supported me throughout its creation. Christoph Leibold shared his photos from Israel with me, and Dieter Mayr images from the Passion in 2010 and 2022. Thank you, Amen Gestaltung, for the great cover and design (and for your name, which seems like it was invented especially for this book).

Thank you to my family, who always gave me the freedom to write and always encouraged me to keep going. Thank you, Emma, for the camel idea. Thank you, Anton, for laughing with me. Thank you, Robert, for your encouragement, for enduring moods and reading over and over again. My children believe that you are only a "real" author if you have written at least two books. But this is a start.

SOURCES

Jörg Adolph: Die Oberammergauer Leidenschaft, if... Productions for Bayerischer Rundfunk, 2010

Jörg Adolph: Die große Passion – Hinter den Kulissen von Oberammergau, if... Productions/Bayerischer Rundfunk, 2012

Gunda Bartels: "Ostern, das heißt Farbe bekennen", in: Der Tagesspiegel, Berlin, 9 April 2020

Hannes Burger: "Uns wär's lieber, wenn's die Preißn gwesen warn", in: Süddeutsche Zeitung, Munich, 16/17/18 May 1970

Hannes Burger: Mit Leidenschaft Passion gespielt, in: Süddeutsche Zeitung, Munich, 16 August 1977

Joseph Alois Daisenberger: Dorfchronik (based on an unknown writer), 1858/1859

Richard Dill: Spielerwahl in Oberammergau, Bayerischer Rundfunk, 1959

Lion Feuchtwanger: Oberammergau, 1910, in: Lion Feuchtwanger: Ein Buch für meine Freunde, Frankfurt am Main, 1984

Ludwig Ganghofer: Brief an Hugo von Hofmannsthal, 1900, in: Holzheimer/Tworek/Woyke (eds.): Leiden schafft Passionen – Oberammergau und sein Spiel, Munich, 2000

Gemeinde Oberammergau: Das Oberammergauer Passionsspiel 1960, Textbuch, Mit Benutzung der alten Texte verfasst von J. A. Daisenberger, Offizieller Gesamttext, für das Jahr 1960 überarbeitet und neu herausgegeben von der Gemeinde Oberammergau, 1960

Gemeinde Oberammergau: Pressetext zur Passion 2000, in: Holzheimer/Tworek/Woyke (eds.): Leiden schafft Passionen – Oberammergau und sein Spiel, Munich, 2000

Mel Gibson: The Passion of the Christ, 2004

Otto Guggenbichler: Oberammergauer Passionsspiele, Bayerischer Rundfunk, 1960

Leopold Höhl: Führer zum Ammergauer Passionsspiel im Jahre 1880, Woerl's Reise-Handbücher, Würzburg, c. 1880

Gerd Holzheimer: Kraglfing oder Wahnmoching – Auseinandersetzung um die Moderne, in: Holzheimer/Tworek/Woyke (eds.): Leiden schafft Passionen – Oberammergau und sein Spiel, Munich, 2000

Otto Huber: Die Erlösung spielen, 1990, quoted in: Holzheimer/Tworek/Woyke (eds.): Leiden schafft Passionen – Oberammergau und sein Spiel, Munich, 2000, p. 13f

Andrea Kammhuber/Petra Wiegers: Der fromme Rebell – Christian Stückl und die Passionsspiele in Oberammergau, Bayerischer Rundfunk, 2018

Joseph Krauskopf: A Rabbi's Impressions of the Oberammergau Passion Play, 1901

Daniel Krochmalnik: Oberammergau – eine deutsche Passion, 1990, in: Holzheimer/Tworek/Woyke (eds.): Leiden schafft Passionen – Oberammergau und sein Spiel, Munich, 2000

Joachim Kronsbein/Bettina Musall: "Draht nach oben", in: Der Spiegel, Hamburg, no. 29, 2005

Hans Lamm: Oberammergau – ein Trauerspiel, 1970, in: Holzheimer/Tworek/Woyke (eds.): Leiden schafft Passionen – Oberammergau und sein Spiel, Munich, 2000

Anton Lang: Aus meinem Leben, Munich, 1930

Theodor Lessing: Oberammergau. Epilog eines Ewig-Malkontenten, 1910, in: Holzheimer/Tworek/Woyke (eds.): Leiden schafft Passionen – Oberammergau und sein Spiel, Munich, 2000

Oliver Mayer-Rüth: Bayerische Passion im Heiligen Land, Bayerischer Rundfunk, 2009

John Warwick Montgomery: Oberammergau – Probleme der Passionsspiele 2010, in: MBS Texte 157, Munich, 2010

Monty Python: The Life of Brian, 1979

Pier Paolo Pasolini: The Gospel According to St. Matthew, 1964

PETA press release, 5 September 2019

Julia Prosinger/Susanne Kippenberger: "Jesus war mir nicht vergönnt" – Wie Christian Stückl den Wahnsinn in Oberammergau organisiert, in: Tagesspiegel, Berlin, 1 February 2020

Milo Rau: The New Gospel, 2021

Andreas Richter, Podcast Mitgehört/Zugehört, episode 12: Osterspecial mit Andreas Richter, Erzbischöfliches Jugendamt München und Freising, www.eja-muenchen.de, 2021

Sven Ricklefs: Christian Stückl – Portrait, in: Anke Roeder/Sven Ricklefs: Regie im Theater – Junge Regisseure, Frankfurt am Main, 1994

Christopher Schmidt: Eroberung im Sturm, in: Sabine Dultz (ed.): Die Münchner Kammerspiele, Munich, Vienna, 2001

Christian Stückl: 2000 – das 40. Spieljahr der Oberammergauer Passion, in: Gemeinde Oberammergau (ed.): Passion 2000, Munich, London, New York, 2000

C. Bernd Sucher: Aus Unterammergau kommt nicht einmal der Esel, in: Süddeutsche Zeitung, Munich, 23 May 2000

C. Bernd Sucher: Eine gottgefällige Lust, in: Süddeutsche Zeitung, Munich, 29 August 2000

Charu Suri: Oberammergau, Germany, 52 Places to Go in 2020, in: New York Times, New York, 2020

Kati Thielitz: Das Spiel seines Lebens, in: Frankfurter Allgemeine Sonntagszeitung, Frankfurt, 25 April 2010

Luis Trenker: Das Wunder von Oberammergau, Gütersloh, Neuauflage 1979

Ilja Trojanow/Richard F. Burton: Oberammergau – Zu Besuch bei den Passionsspielen, Zurich, 2010

Hermann Unterstöger: Die Leidensgeschichte einer Versöhnung, in: Süddeutsche Zeitung, Munich, 17/18 May 1980

Hermann Unterstöger: "Wirf zum heiligen Staunen dich nieder", in: Süddeutsche Zeitung, Munich, 21 May 1984

Hermann Unterstöger: Kaiphas' Sohn als Spielleiter, in: Süddeutsche Zeitung, Munich, 11/12 July 1987

Hermann Unterstöger: Ein bayrisch-katholisches Glaubenszeugnis, in: Süddeutsche Zeitung, Munich, 21 May 1990

Angelika Winterer (ed.): Das Gelübde und die "Gründungsurkunde" des Oberammergauer Passionsspiels, Munich, 2020

Josef Georg Ziegler: Das Oberammergauer Passionsspiel. Erbe und Auftrag, in: Holzheimer/Tworek/Woyke (eds.): Leiden schafft Passionen – Oberammergau und sein Spiel, Munich, 2000

www.passionsspiele-oberammergau.de/de/spiel/historie

All quotes not otherwise cited are taken from conversations that the author conducted between 2019 and 2021 with David Bender, Ulrike Bubenzer, Kilian Clauß, Stefan Hageneier, Cengiz Görür, Markus Köpf, Monika Lang, Carsten Lück, Frederik Mayet, Ludwig Mödl, Anton Preisinger, Eva Reiser, Andreas Richter, Andreas Rödl, Rochus Rückel, Toni Scholler, Sophie Schuster, Alexander Schwarz, Christoph Stöger, Lorenz Stöger, Christian Stückl, Peter Stückl and Markus Zwink.
The author Monika Lang provided access to the court files of the 1990 proceedings regarding equal rights for women.

NOTES

[1] Höhl 1880: 7f

[2] Trojanow 2010: 8f

[3] Trojanow/Burton 2010: 65f

[4] Lang 1930: 118

[5] Lang 1930: 143

[6] Lang 1930: 144

[7] Lang 1930: 145

[8] Feuchtwanger 1910: 238

[9] Ziegler 1990: 35

[10] Ziegler 2000: 35

[11] Stückl 2000: 12

[12] Sucher: 29.08.2000

[13] Holzheimer 2000: 14

[14] www.passionsspiele-oberammergau.de/de/spiel/historie

[15] Daisenberger 1858

[16] Winterer 2020

[17] Daisenberger 1858

[18] Daisenberger 1858

[19] Lang 1930: 118

[20] Lang 1930: 123f

[21] Trenker 1979: 6

[22] Ziegler 2000: 36

[23] Adolph 2010

[24] Kammhuber/Wiegers 2018

[25] Ziegler 2000: 36

[26] Sucher 23.5.2000

[27] Trojanow/Burton 2010: 67

[28] Feuchtwanger 1910: 239

[29] Krochmalnik 1990: 160

[30] Trojanow/Burton 2010: 80f

[31] Lessing 1910: 31

[32] Ganghofer 1900: 23

[33] Burger 1970

[34] Matthäus 27, 25

[35] Gemeinde Oberammergau 1960: 117

[36] Adolph 2010

[37] Krauskopf 1901

[38] Feuchtwanger 1910: 233ff

[39] Lamm 1970: 170

[40] Lamm 1970: 171

[41] www.passionsspiele-oberammergau.de/de/spiel/historie

[42] Burger 1970

[43] Burger 1970

[44] Burger 1970

[45] Burger 1977

[46] cf. Adolph 2010

[47] Unterstöger 1980

[48] Unterstöger 1980

[49] Unterstöger 1984

[50] Unterstöger 1987

[51] Unterstöger 1987

[52] Kronsbein/Musall 2005

[53] Unterstöger 1990

[54] Schmidt 2001: 382

[55] Gemeinde Oberammergau 2000

[56] Ricklefs 1994: 59

[57] Sucher 23.5.2000

[58] Kronsbein/Musall 2005

[59] Adolph 2010

[60] Thielitz 2010

[61] Montgomery 2010: 3

[62] Montgomery 2010: 4

[63] Montgomery 2010: 6

[64] Mayer-Rüth 2009

[65] cf. Mayer-Rüth 2009

[66] Lang 1930: 18

[67] Adolph 2010

[68] Adolph 2010

[69] cf. Adolph 2010

[70] cf. Mayer-Rüth 2009

[71] Mayer-Rüth 2009

[72] Mayer-Rüth 2009

[73] Trojanow/Burton 2010: 62

[74] Lang 1930: 21

[75] Richter 2021

[76] Lang 1930: 19

[77] Trojanow/Burton 2010: 119

[78] Trojanow/Burton 2010: 119

[79] Lang 1930: 27f

[80] Prosinger/Kippenberger 2020

[81] Kammhuber/Wiegers 2018

[82] Richter 2021

[83] Dill 1959

[84] Dill 1959

[85] Lang 1930: 111

[86] Lang 1930: 44f

[87] Lang 1930: 27

[88] Lang 1930: 127/132

[89] Richter 2021

[90] Presseerklärung PETA 2019

[91] Lang 1930: 60

[92] Lang 1930: 110f

[93] Richter 2021

[94] Trojanow/Burton 2010: 68f

[95] Holzheimer 2000: 10

[96] Huber 1990: 13f

[97] Mayer-Rüth 2009

[98] Mayer-Rüth 2009

[99] Bartels 2020

The Author

Anne Fritsch was born in 1978. She studied theatre studies, German literature and Jewish history at LMU Munich followed by cultural criticism at Theaterakademie August Everding. As a student she assisted at the Münchner Volkstheater and the Münchner Kammerspiele. She lives with her family in Munich and works as an author and cultural journalist, appearing in a range of specialist publications, as well as the *Frankfurter Allgemeine Sonntagszeitung*, the *taz* and the *Süddeutsche Zeitung*. She works as a freelance editor and Munich correspondent for *Deutsche Bühne* and *Junge Bühne*.